MASTERING CONTEMPORARY
JEWELRY DESIGN

MASTERING CONTEMPORARY
JEWELRY DESIGN

LORETTA LAM

Inspiration, Process, and Finding Your Voice

SCHIFFER
PUBLISHING

4880 Lower Valley Road • Atglen, PA 19310

Other Schiffer Books on Related Subjects:

Drawing for Jewelers: Master Class in Professional Design, Maria Josep Forcadell Berenguer and Josep Asunción Pastor, ISBN 978-0-7643-4058-1

The Art of Jewelry Design: Principles of Design, Rings & Earrings, Maurice P. Galli, Dominique Rivière & Fanfan Li, ISBN 978-0-88740-562-4

Narrative Jewelry: Tales from the Toolbox, Mark Fenn, Foreword by Jack Cunningham, PhD, ISBN 978-0-7643-5414-4

ISBN: 978-0-7643-5919-4
Printed in China

Published by Schiffer Publishing, Ltd.
4880 Lower Valley Road
Atglen, PA 19310
Phone: (610) 593-1777; Fax: (610) 593-2002
E-mail: Info@schifferbooks.com
Web: www.schifferbooks.com

For our complete selection of fine books on this and related subjects, please visit our website at www.schifferbooks.com. You may also write for a free catalog.

Schiffer Publishing's titles are available at special discounts for bulk purchases for sales promotions or premiums. Special editions, including personalized covers, corporate imprints, and excerpts, can be created in large quantities for special needs. For more information, contact the publisher.

We are always looking for people to write books on new and related subjects. If you have an idea for a book, please contact us at proposals@schifferbooks.com.

I DWELL IN POSSIBILITY.

—EMILY DICKINSON

CONTENTS

ACKNOWLEDGMENTS

Writing this book has been a solitary job. Just me and the computer and piles of reference material. But I really didn't do it alone. I want to thank all of my teachers and students, colleagues and friends, and all the members of my artistic tribe who encouraged the germination of an idea to send out roots, grow, and flower into this book.

A big, juicy hug to all the artists who participated in the project, generously lending your images, thoughts, and suggestions. Through your artistic endeavors, you lead the way, blazing new trails and inspiring us all with the wonders you create. Thanks to everyone at Schiffer Publishing, especially Sandra Korinchak, for understanding my vision and bringing it to fruition.

I could not have done the job without the help of some very special friends: Alix, Denise, Robin, Emily, Lynne, and Barb, who were my constant companions offering advice and assistance, support and discernment, an ear or a shoulder—whatever I needed to continue on the journey. And of course my soul sister, sidekick, doula, and partner in crime Ronna Sarvas Weltman, who walked with me, hand in hand, every step of the way. This book is our achievement. I'm grateful and proud of what we have accomplished.

Most of all, thanks to my husband and son, Gary and Jake. Like a lot of people, I need to talk through my projects and challenges and this one created an almost non-stop, stream-of-consciousness chatter. Thanks for continuing to ask me how the book was going . . . because you knew once I started talking it would be a while before I stopped. I love you guys . . . and your little dog too!

INTRODUCTION
How to Use This Book

Recently my husband and I embarked on a DIY home improvement project to install crown molding. How hard could it be, right?

He would hold the piece of molding up along the ceiling as we tried to decide how to make the end cut. There was a lot of talk . . . "I think it should go like this [hand gestures]," "No, cut it like that [more gestures]," and "This part definitely has to go like this and be cut like that!" You get the idea. Neither one of us had the vocabulary needed to communicate about the subject. It was very ineffective and caused a good deal of frustration for both of us.

Mastery of the concepts and vocabulary of design helps us express ourselves as jewelry artists, improves our ability to solve creative problems or to get help when we're stuck, and, of course, helps us grow. If you don't know what a particular tool can do, you will use it either inefficiently or incorrectly. Likewise, you may have extensive technical skills, but without the ability to express your thoughts and feelings, your artistic growth will be restricted. This book is essentially a how-to book. It will help you learn how to choose the applicable principles and elements of design.

It will show you how to find your inspiration and your voice. It will teach you how to develop your process and the ability to give and receive critique.

This book is the go-to design reference guide for jewelry makers at all levels, regardless of medium. Are you a jewelry hobbyist, student, or craft entrepreneur looking for answers to your design dilemmas? Are you a workshop teacher who wants to offer your students more than techniques, helping them grow as artists, or a gallerist looking for more powerful ways to communicate with buyers? Wherever you are in the jewelry world, I hope this book will inspire you, make you curious, enrich and deepen your understanding, and help you develop as a jewelry artist.

This book contains a lot of information, but it's easily managed. Take your time reading it. If you are a front-to-back reader, give each topic time to sink in. Are you more of a hands-on learner? Use it as a workbook and do the exercises, working through each chapter in an active way. You might also hopscotch around the book, choosing topics according to your needs. Not everyone is as interested in color as I am!

However you choose to read this book, I know it will inspire you. Between these covers are over 125 gorgeous images of every kind of contemporary jewelry, created by artists from all over the world. From driftwood to high-carat gold, from string to sterling, what they have in common is great design. The images will speak to you and tell you the story of their makers. Each time you pick this book up, you will see something new, be reminded of something you already knew but forgot, and pick up another crucial tidbit about design.

Throughout my career as a working artist, whether I was selling, teaching, or writing about jewelry, my mission has always been to share the valuable lessons about art and design that I learned in art school. As I sat writing this book, you were on my mind. Throughout the process of gathering and collating the information, I thought about your concerns and questions and tried my best to give you clear, concise direction. This book is an expression of my gratitude for the jewelry community, which has been so supportive and has added intrinsic value to my life. It is intended to help you move along your artistic path. I hope you enjoy the journey.

Loretta Lam. "Leaves" brooches. Polymer with nickel pin backs. 2017. Artist photo.

PART ONE

GETTING STARTED

How do we begin to design jewelry? Whether you are an art student or have been making jewelry for years, or whether you make your living through your art or simply enjoy the occasional weekend, it makes no difference to the creative process. All artists are on the same journey—learning, experimenting, growing, getting stuck, and having to start again. It is the nature of art and the people who make things.

There's an old saying: "Everything is created twice—first in the mind and then in the world." It's true—the journey begins with an idea. Inspiration is the essential first step for all creative endeavors. Discover what you are curious about, what moves you, and what you want to say to the world. Finding your unique inspiration is like tapping into your personal archeology. It takes a little digging and you will get dirty, but it is essential to uncover your personal motivation.

Once an idea has formed in the mind, your artistic process is the series of steps you take to find the best version of that idea. This ritual behavior is a crucial part of the journey. Choosing and gathering materials, deciding what to emphasize, arranging and rearranging component parts, and coming up with a construction plan; all this and more becomes your process. As part of that process you must also consider function. Understanding issues of weight, mass, safety, and durability will help you design the very best jewelry.

So Young Park. "Dreaming Tree" necklace. Oxidized silver, sapphires, various stones. 2015. Artist photo.

INSPIRATION

Jewelry design doesn't begin with making. It begins with a spark of inspiration, something you have experienced—a thought, feeling, or concept. It begins with the ephemeral something that catches your interest but can dissipate with the lightest breeze. This is the most personal part of the journey. The work you make is the work only you can make, because it's all about you. The way you experience the world. What you love and hate, what excites you, and what repels you. Only you can find out where your inspiration lies.

There are two steps to finding your inspiration. First, you must stay open. That means paying attention to what makes your heart flutter, what keeps pulling you back, and what you are curious about. Start to notice what attracts you, and record it for future reference. Noticing the inspiration around you is a practice. The more you do it, the better you get at recognizing the things that get your attention and spark your creativity.

While the first part of finding your inspiration is drawing things to you, the second part is keeping things out. I call this "banishing the shoulds." This means standing guard against your own limiting beliefs. It's when you hear that judgmental voice in your head telling you what you should and should not do. "That's not art! Don't do that. That's a bad idea! Who do you think you are anyway?" When you hear these things, it's time to close the door and banish them! Your inner critic doesn't know what you are capable of and neither do you, until you try it.

Ask five artists what inspires them to create, and you'll get at least five answers . . . maybe ten. But most people fall into two categories. Those with external focus are inspired by the world around us. Travel,

Artist Myung Urso:

With the arrival of autumn my mind often travels far away to the scenery of the golden-colored rice fields of my hometown in my native country of South Korea. The neckpiece "October" is a piece that was created in 2009, three years after I left the country and moved to upstate New York. Imagining the contrast of smooth and soft landscape of ripened rice fields surrounded by mountains expresses my nostalgia through the use of stiffened threads and hand-dyed silk. The photo of this landscape scenery was taken during my father's funeral service with my iPhone camera. The dazzling harvest season once again caught my eyes. The scenery was too beautiful in contrast with the sadness of my family's loss. My memory goes back to the period of time when I was little, being with my mom and my sister; we were in the middle of the golden rice field catching grasshoppers. Now my late parents are placed looking at the same scenery from their eternal place.

Myung Urso. "October" pendant. Silk, thread, amber, beads, silver, and lacquer. 2009. Photo: Tim J. Fuss.

people, cultures, nature, politics, and space. These artists get their juice from what they perceive of the world, and their creations are their internal response to it. The second group of artists is internally focused. These people get their most significant inspiration from their own hearts and minds. Their internal world is rich and complex and full of ideas that they need to express. Which camp do you fall into? Maybe some of both?

To find your true path, you need to do a little personal archeology. Look deep inside to find the answers to some personal questions. What do you cherish or revere? What makes you feel vital and alive? What provokes you? What moves you—physically, spiritually, and emotionally? What drives you? What brings you true joy—cooking, working out, music, meditation, reading, sports? Expand your awareness to your own story, talents, interests, and fascinations, all those things that make you who you are.

Collect the stuff you love—photos, ideas, songs, flavors. Keep a journal or sketchbook with you to capture ideas and impressions when they happen. Some of our best ideas occur to us in random places, such as the grocery store or the dog park. Make note of them right away so they don't disappear. Take photos or rip them out of magazines. Collect these items in a journal or folder. You will want to study them later to look for spheres of interest and commonalities among your ideas. Keep the pad and pencil next to the bed. Then, when inspiration wakes you up, you can catch it before it's gone. Take the pad with you when you're working. Ideas for the next project will undoubtedly come to you when you are working on the current design, and you need to write them down.

Make it a habit to record the emotional, spiritual, and visual experiences you have every day. Some days it will take only a couple of minutes—a description of textures or a quick sketch of shape relationships. Develop the habit of capturing these bits of inspiration. If you practice every day, it will be easier to access your creativity.

Artist Beverly Tadeu:

Most of my creations are inspired by nature: beautifully arched and layered branches, twisting tendrils of roots, varied surfaces and textures. Nature is spontaneous, with surprises of asymmetry within the symmetry of form. I am constantly looking at the structure of things, why something has caught my eye, what causes me to pause and look closer, what makes me sigh with delight. I try to bring these elements into my work. When working on a complicated piece, I will often develop the ideas over a series of days, sometimes weeks, letting the design unfold, finding new inspirations within the composition as I move forward.

Many of my art jewelry pieces express intimate or more global thoughts and ideas. Our fragility and strength are expressed through the delicate wires bound together to create sturdy sculptural objects. My rooted series was created at a time I was in transition from years of living abroad, getting used to being back in the United States. I felt unmoored, adrift, unrooted. This work was an expression of the need to find roots in my life, a metaphorical translation of wanting to be at home.

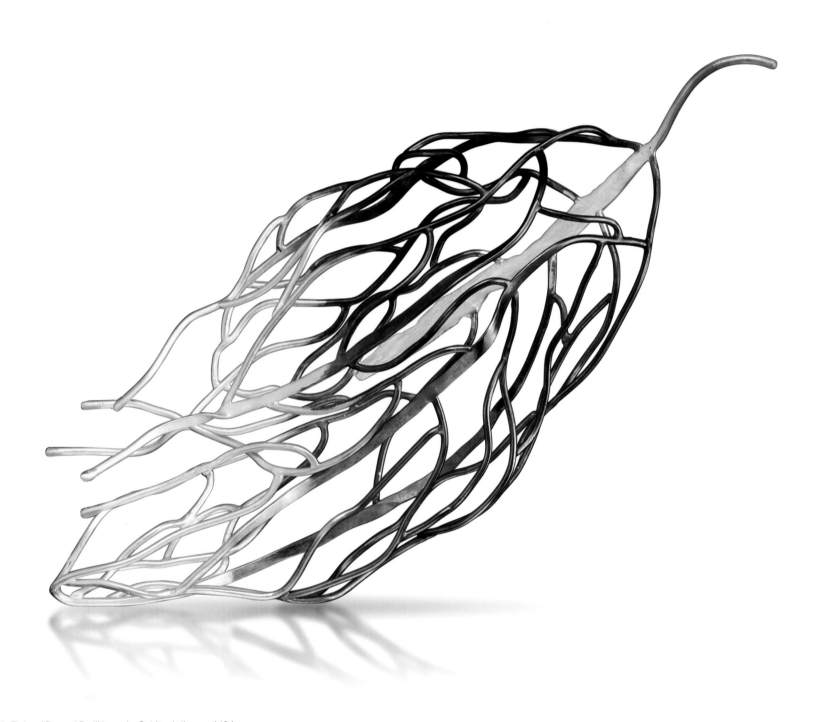

Beverly Tadeu. "Rooted Pod" brooch. Oxidized silver and 18 kt. gold. 2009. Photo: Hap Sakwa.

ACCESS YOUR INSPIRATION

Feeling closed off? Can't find a new or compelling idea? Try these ideas for getting unstuck.

Change up your routine. Live your day backward.

Daydream. Fill a few pages of your sketchbook with shapes, words, song lyrics, feelings, ideas.

Go into your studio or workspace and see what happens.

Do busy work or clean your studio. Rework old pieces you aren't happy with.

Get up and dance. Go for a walk or get some exercise.

"Sharpen the saw." Look at your sketchbooks for past design ideas you never tried.

Artist Amy Tavern:

Observation is the act of noticing. As a resident in a new and foreign place, Antwerp, Belgium, my power of observation became important in unusual and unexpected ways. It heightened in a way that allowed me to see more. Over the course of two months I recorded my daily observations in photographs, drawings, and text, capturing all the things I had never seen before. The daily commute from my apartment to my studio was on a tram. One morning as it zoomed along the street, I saw someone standing in a window, looking out. There she was observing from an open second-story window. I saw this person only for a moment, and in another moment we were gone in two different directions. I wondered about her for a long time, about observing her existence. I re-created that moment in a brass-and-silver brooch that suggests the act of opening the window and looking out, as well as the presence of a person. Further, the combination of different metals provides contrast and allows for patinas that mimic the aged surfaces of most of the buildings in the city.

Amy Tavern. "In Passing" brooch. Sterling silver and brass. 2012. Photo: Victor Darmont.

Artist Donna Veverka:

I am inspired by the mystery and faded glory of ancient architectural fragments and the cultures they represent. Visiting ruins kept "in situ" is to experience history viscerally. It is like time travel—you see where they were built, feel the textures of what remains, and sense the awesome scale. My interest is in how we view these ancient survivors of once-powerful civilizations and the monumental architecture reduced through the ages to a pile of rubble.

I began to reflect on how modern civilization displays these remarkable objects of the past. They are strapped into place, piled neatly, or carefully displayed in museums. I am attracted to the pins, straps, and metal connections that are strong enough to hold the marble together. But I purposefully leave my fragments in the state that time has left them. I create scars and breaks in the marble, distressing them, and oxidize the sterling to give it a feeling of the ages. I hope the pieces tell a story about the past and about the rise and fall of some of the greatest builders in history. I want to engage the viewer in the mystery of what time has done to shape these giants into what we see today.

Donna Veverka. "Ancient Rubble" necklace. Sterling silver, hand-carved marble. 2012. Photo: Robert Diamante.

PROCESS

Process is how we get from inspiration to a finished piece of jewelry. It is the artistic routine or set of steps we use to realize our ideas. This plan will help you work out design concerns, find construction solutions, and generate ideas for future projects. Process is individual and aligns with your creative personality. There is no right or wrong method—whatever suits you and helps you get from start to finish is your process. Many artists create a transitional ritual to begin their process: putting on certain clothes, traveling to the studio, or organizing their workspace in a particular way. Creating a transitional space allows for the paradigm shift we must make to get from our day-to-day life to our creative zone.

Getting good at making art depends on how you train that part of your brain. Your process is that training and will evolve over time. As our artistic skills mature, our decision-making ability is sharpened and it becomes easier to recognize what is working. We are more facile, able to quickly change course and adjust the design. As your mastery of the process grows, things get easier.

Creativity is all about problem-solving. The act of making something from nothing is remarkable.

Artist Chris Carpenter:

My jewelry pieces are quite sculptural and start from drawings and models in cardboard and wire.

The sketches are mostly abstract shapes, not too exacting and sometimes quite vague. From there I take elements out and develop the shapes in three dimensions. During this stage I can see how I am going to make it in metal. Often I come back to old drawings and see other shapes in them. The ideas are constantly developing and changing.

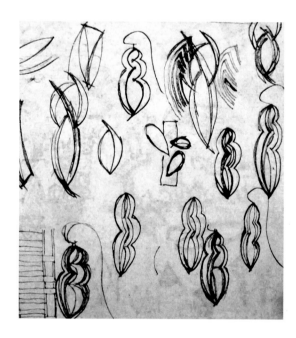

Chris Carpenter. "Arches" earrings. Sterling silver. 2018. Artist photo.

Whether your problems are technical or aesthetic, thinking ahead and coming up with possible solutions is essential. Drawing is a good place to start. It is the artist's version of practicing musical scales. It's a way of capturing ideas; visual note-taking and recording cues to stimulate memory and spark imagination. Drawing helps us communicate with teachers, peers, and customers. Drawing helps resolve problems before they come up, as well as working through variations of a design to find the best solution. It gives us a place to store concepts for the future, without relying on memory. Then, when the creative doldrums hit, our sketchbooks offer new directions.

People often have a negative reaction to drawing; perhaps they were harshly judged as children. Maybe they perpetuate that judgment even now. If this sounds familiar, break away from the fear by drawing often and not worrying about how well you do it. If you picked up an instrument you've never played, it will sound bad for a long time. It takes practice. Your sketchbook is for you alone. It's never going to be published or put on display. It's an important and helpful skill, so banish the negative thoughts and practice. Make your sketchbook a place to collect ideas. Fill it with photos you've taken or images from a magazine. Capture bits of color, texture, form, and shapes, all the things that inspire you. Then organize these bits of information to use in the next piece.

Many artists prefer a three-dimensional approach called model making or 3-D sketching. This involves making mockups of your ideas as quick impressions of the design. It helps to envision how the piece will look when complete, and points out possible construction issues before they arise. If your work is sculptural, this approach could be for you.

Finally there is a process called "action and response." This process takes you into your studio to start experimenting directly with your materials. You find out how the material reacts to your ideas, and find solutions under the direct influence of the material's strengths and limitations. Many artists who create this way end up with a box of component parts that weren't quite successful but are instructional for future designs. It is important, if you work this way, to be able to stop in the midst of the process if things aren't going well. Don't finish everything you start. Some designs need to be put aside.

Artist Sydney Lynch:

I love being out of doors in every type of landscape, and I love to travel. Like many artists, I find nature to be the ultimate source of inspiration—an enormous, ever-changing repository of shapes, lines, patterns, and colors. I rarely make jewelry that is a direct reference to something I've photographed. Design is a more subtle, complex process of adding images to my own mental "hard drive" and having them slowly combine, percolate, and find their way into my work. Once I have the initial idea, I try to draw quickly and spontaneously to capture a natural, instinctive shape and line. While I do go back and fine-tune the drawing, I've found that it's better not to labor over a design, or the original inspiration can be lost.

Balance is the key to a successful design, and color is very important in my work too. Stones have a lot to do with my design decisions, and I'm equally thoughtful about combining the colors and shapes of gemstones in a piece. Proportions of line and shape have to be carefully considered for the design to work; a slight change can affect the resolution of the design.

Sydney Lynch. Frame brooch. Faceted labradorite and tourmalines, 22 kt. gold and oxidized silver. Photo: Alan Jackson.

THE BASIC STEPS OF MAKING

Play: actions that do not have objectives—sketch, snap photos, build models

Imagine: attaining a concrete, though perhaps abstract, vision of the design

Set limitations: apply rules that assist design by limiting choices

Problem-solving: anticipate, identify, consider, and structure solutions

Create: design, arrange, assemble, and repeat

Revise: edit, move and remove, improve

Artist Loretta Lam:

My work begins with color. Something beautiful catches my attention: something in nature, a work of art, or a picture in a magazine. I take that inspiration and start to work on the palette. I define and refine the colors directly in my medium. I try to infuse the polymer with mood and memories, a sense of place and time. This is the most exciting part of the process for me. Everything is possible, and there are no problems or issues yet. I use my sketchbook to work out the shapes, patterns, and textures.

I make notes too; about the music that's on, or the book I'm reading—whatever is currently feeding my soul. I work through the construction steps and try to anticipate the whole process of making the piece. Although the visual inspiration may come from walking the dog in the woods, everything else comes from deep inside me. I do all the psychological work before I start to make the piece. Then I'm back in a creative problem-solving mode—but I know where I'm going.

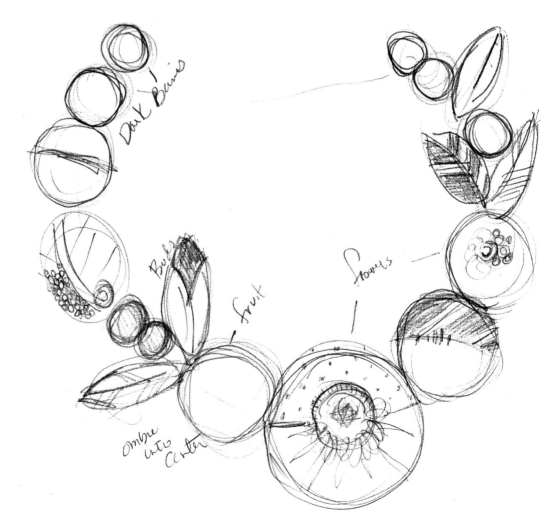

Loretta Lam. "Kisses Sweeter Than Wine" necklace. Polymer
and glass spacers. 2015. Photo: Bob Barrett.

One of the best reasons to keep journals, sketchbooks, photos, models, and components is to have a resource, to find a new direction, or to revisit an old idea. Reviewing your own archives is instructive and connects you back to what you long to express.

Your process is individually tailored to your creative temperament. Do you get ideas at odd hours or in unusual places? Does your inspiration come from specific external sources? Then your process will include capturing images and ideas in a sketchbook or with a camera. Are you more likely to work in a mess of components and materials? Do you get in conversations with your medium, allowing the interplay to direct the design? Then your process is more three-dimensional, action and response. Understanding your process will lead you to create more personal work, find your own path, and be more fully engaged with your jewelry design.

Artist Clare Hillerby:

On a brief trip to London, I wandered the streets to photograph graffiti, derelict buildings, old and worn shop signs, and textures from the urban environment. I collect ephemera along the way and make sketches and collage them with pieces of old papers. These collages, doodles, and notes inform my designs and suggest where to begin with the metal. After these preliminary sketches, I make various metal components. This allows me to play with different combinations of the metalwork and ephemeral fragments. This process goes back and forth until elements are selected for the final composition and construction can begin.

Clare Hillerby. "Walthamstow to B'ham" brooch. Silver, postcards, photograph, linen map, perspex, gold. 2012. Artist photo.

Functional Considerations

Throughout history and across cultures, jewelry has been permitted or forbidden on the basis of gender, class, and occupation. It has served as a talisman imbued with special powers for healing or for keeping the bogeyman away. It has been a conduit of wealth and an emblem identifying the owner's social position as royalty or cleric.

Makers of jewelry were categorized as craftsmen and artisans until very recently, when there was a shift in how jewelers see themselves and their work. While the term "fine art" typically applies to work that carries an intellectual and emotional sensibility without any particular function, contemporary jewelry infuses these aesthetic ideals into objects that are off the wall and on the human body. This is a radical shift from the ornamental concerns of the artisan. Jewelry is now regarded as a vehicle of expression for the artist, who is able to engage with his or her subject through the use of art principles, symbolism, and conceptual exploration. There is also the desire to challenge and change preconceived notions about jewelry. By breaking away from historical constraints, contemporary jewelry has earned a rightful place in the fine-art world.

Although we now approach design from an art-directed point of view, we must still address function. Along with beauty and originality, the designer must consider comfort, safety, material selection, and durability. Function isn't everything, but it is an important part of your design process.

Weight considerations are initially addressed by the choice of medium. The weight of a piece of silver jewelry will be quite different from a similar piece made of paper or fiber. The fiber artist has virtually no weight restrictions, while size restrictions are more likely based on bulk, durability, and style. Bulk refers to the total volume of the piece of jewelry and how much space the piece takes up. Large-scale jewelry is the current trend, so if you work in heavier materials, look for ways to keep the bulk while cutting the weight. Weight is a relative term, and people have very distinct preferences when it comes to bulk and weight. This is especially true in earrings.

Rigidity and flexibility are also part of the weight issue. A lot of weight can be deferred by designs created in flexible materials. Imagine a cuff bracelet that twists easily into position, compared with a stiff cuff that must be forced on at the wrist. Even if the two items are roughly the same weight, the flexible piece will be easier to wear. Jump rings, hinges, ball joints, rivets, and chain are mechanical devices that help distribute weight and make rigid materials more flexible and easier to wear.

Safety is an issue in most jewelry media. Metals, found objects, and some alternative materials can have pointy bits and sharp edges. These things must be avoided to protect the wearer or anyone who gets close to them. Avoid hooks or barbs and any shapes that snag or stick, to prevent possible damage to clothing. Be conscious of craftsmanship. Make the highest-quality work you can, and always strive to improve your skills so that all elements are smooth and secure. This will help safeguard your work and your customer.

Durability is a function of good craftsmanship as well as medium. You don't want your jewelry to dissolve in the rain, crumble in the cold, or crack at the slightest bump. If you work in breakable materials such as ceramics or glass, be sure that you understand all the parameters of the media and have mastered them. What can you do to make the material stronger? Are there forms you shouldn't use or techniques to avoid? If you work in fibers or paper, are there ways to support the media to give it additional strength? Are there processes that will weatherproof your jewelry to increase durability? Whatever your medium, will it hold up to regular, normal usage or is it simply too fragile?

After considering the weight of the item, flexibility of the material, any potentially hazardous protrusions, and durability, you should also consider external circumstances. How and where will the piece be worn? Can the owner work or type while wearing that ring or bracelet? Does that necklace or brooch function with an overcoat? Are those earrings too long to hang properly on the wearer? There is a time and place for jewelry that does not conform to these conditions, and of course you are free to make that choice. But if you do so, do it with intention and awareness of the consequences. In almost all situations, we are making jewelry to be worn. The process is incomplete until the design is purchased and worn by others. If it doesn't function for their lifestyle, it will sit in a drawer. Nobody wants that!

Art Smith. "Modern Cuff" copper and brass. Ca. 1950. Gift of Charles L. Russell, Brooklyn Museum. 2007. Photo: Dwayne Resnick.

FUNCTIONAL CONCERNS FOR EACH JEWELRY TYPE

BROOCHES

Jewelry makers love to make brooches. They are small-scale sculptural pieces that allow for more creative freedom and exist in the prime real estate of the lapel area. The area is flat and asexual, so people can get a good look at your work without appearing inappropriate.

When designing brooches, be conscious of depth. If it stands out too far, it will affect the way the piece hangs and is more likely to get damaged or harm clothing.

Consider the center of the gravity of the piece. The traditional position for a pin stem is about a third of the way above the horizontal center. This keeps the brooch from falling forward on the garment. If you have a top-heavy design or one with an unusual shape, try using a vertical pin stem or two tie tacks to help distribute the weight. Remember, people will pick up a brooch and turn it over to look at the back. Take care to design the back of a brooch and treat it with the same craftsmanship as the front.

EARRINGS

Earrings must be lightweight but they don't need to match. If you make asymmetrical earrings, the weight should be the same. Asymmetrical earrings are an excellent way to stretch your creativity and use your new design knowledge.

There are three basic kinds of earrings: posts, hoops, and drop earrings. Post earrings sit on the ear and are well supported on the earlobe. Logically it would seem that they could be much bigger. The truth is that large post earrings are often less flattering. Be sure to analyze the design in situ.

Careful placement of the post or ear wire will ensure proper distribution of the weight of the earring so that it hangs straight and the earlobe is not pulled or stretched. Try your designs on several people to make sure the earrings hang as desired.

Ear wires must have edges and ends that are soft and rounded to prevent damage to the pierced ear. Larger and heavier earrings should be supported on the ear with a good-sized ear nut, lobe support, or T-back.

The size of an earring is ultimately limited by the physical capacity of the earlobe to hold the earring without tearing. Heavy earrings worn over time may stretch or tear the earlobe.

The purpose of earrings is to draw attention to a woman's most beautiful feature—her eyes, mouth, or neck. When designing earrings, consider which feature you are highlighting.

Current adornment trends include earring groups that are not standard pairs. A singular earring can create drama, while multiples expand your design possibilities. Keep functionality at the top of your list and let your imagination go wild.

BRACELETS

Bracelets get a lot of wear and tear because they are worn on the wrist. They get banged against all sorts of surfaces. Durability is a top design consideration. Your bracelet should be strong enough to withstand normal usage, so the wearer feels confident about its strength and resilience.

Consider the center of gravity for your bracelet. A focal element should stay put on the top of the wrist. This can be accomplished through fit, materials, and construction.

Egypt. Earrings with an Atef crown. Gold, stone, and glass. 3rd–2nd century BCE. Gift of Christos G. Bastis, in honor of Philippe de Montebello, 1995. Metropolitan Museum of Art.

A bracelet can be a solid bangle, cuff, or segmented. The type of bracelet is often dependent on your choice of materials, how you want the piece to be viewed, and how much flexibility or drape you desire.

Throughout history, bracelets have been worn at the wrist, ankle, and upper arm. Today, bracelets are most commonly worn at the wrist. You might like to explore these other areas for new design opportunities.

RINGS

Rings are the most unprotected category of jewelry. We're constantly putting our hands in our pockets, doing chores, working, or playing, so we constantly subject our rings to possible damage. High-quality design and craftsmanship are essential for rings to withstand this kind of heavy use.

Ring shanks should be well constructed with smooth edges so they do not cut into fingers. They should also be thin enough to sit nicely between the fingers.

Functional considerations of weight, height, and scale are in force for most rings. Exceptions are made for "cocktail rings." These pieces are designed to be worn when you're not doing anything in particular, except showing off your ring!

PENDANTS

One or two elements strung on flexible material and worn around the neck shouldn't have many functional problems. Proportion is one consideration. Be conscious of the size relationship between the pendant and the stringing material. A 3" circle hung on narrow string would not be visually pleasing. The proportions are wrong.

Pendants can be hung from one point, several points, or a tube component. If your pendant is suspended from a single point, take care of the position because it can flip around when being worn. This is an opportunity for some creative problem-solving. Could you make the pendant reversible? This adds value and interest to a piece.

How long should a pendant be? There's the highly visible area from the base of the neck to the décolletage. This is preferred by many women who don't want to draw attention to their chest. Or choose a longer pendant, hanging below the bustline for a cool, contemporary look. Just steer clear of the bustline; it's unflattering in almost all cases. Pendants 30" and longer will swing when worn. Take care that the piece is not fragile and won't be damaged by everyday use.

NECKLACES

When designing necklaces, think about when and where it will be worn. Is this a casual, everyday piece or something more dramatic, for a special occasion? Is this design more of an accessory or a statement piece? Is it for work, weekends, date night, or a Hollywood premiere? The answers will inform your design choices. The more unique a necklace is, the greater your creative freedom.

Flexibility is a major consideration in necklaces. Rigid designs such as collars or torques have the advantage of staying in place so that your design elements are well displayed. Increasing flexibility by your choice of materials and the use of segments will increase the drape of the piece. This makes for a more elegant wearing experience.

Clasps should coordinate with the overall necklace design. Imagine a unique, artistic, handmade neckpiece and a mass-produced lobster claw clasp. It just doesn't work. Give careful thought to the style and type of clasp

you will need to enhance and elevate the overall design.

Think through the proportion between the necklace parts and the clasp. As with pendants, you don't want the visual harmony thrown off by bad proportion.

MEN'S JEWELRY

Functional considerations do not change when designing accessories for men. You still need to consider weight, safety, flexibility, and durability in your work. Pieces may be a slightly larger scale and therefore marginally heavier. Otherwise the differences will be more stylistic than functional.

Designing Jewelry Sets

Have you considered creating pieces that can be worn together?

This is the way many customers prefer to buy jewelry. They want pieces that work together thematically, and feel more confident knowing the designer has intended the pieces as an ensemble.

If this appeals to you, begin by designing a major necklace.

Let it be the foundation that the other items in the set can riff on.

Repeat motifs, colors, textures, and shapes to create a thread of cohesiveness in the set.

Create pieces that inform and enhance each other and can be worn in a mix-and-match way.

A Word about Commerce

This is not a book about the craft business. There are plenty of good books out there if you're looking for that information. But all creative endeavors have an aspect of the commercial. Selling your work, even if only to friends and family, is a necessary step toward being taken seriously by others and often by ourselves. When you enter the marketplace you must address issues of value. How much is what you do worth? There's nothing like getting paid for something you've made with your own hands. Your hard work deserves to be rewarded with hard-earned money. Then there's the feeling you get when others appreciate your work enough to buy and wear your jewelry.

But how do you manage the discrepancies between your artistic expression and your customer concerns? It seems that whatever choices you make—style or subject matter, scale or color—someone will suggest you alter it. What should you do? How much do you adjust what you want to make to meet market demands? Do you follow trends or stick to your own vision? How do you decide when to say yes and when to say no? There are no right or wrong answers. How you run your business is completely up to you. There are many ways to structure a craft business, and you will need to make decisions and prioritize your goals.

People will offer you all kinds of advice, but only you can decide if other people's suggestions suit your vision for where you want to take your art. There are lots of ways to approach the commercial side of art, and it's up to you to find the best path for you.

Even when creating a commissioned piece and working closely with a customer to design what they want, the final decisions are still yours. You are the creative architect of the work. If, during the design phase, the vision strays too far from your aesthetic, if it becomes unbalanced, disharmonious, or just plain ugly, will you want your name on it? You are in charge. You need to come up with successful alternatives and explain the differences to the client.

When you engage with someone else about your designs, that's the time you need to call on your design expertise the most. You will have the vocabulary to talk about the principles of art that are important to you and what makes some pieces better than others. You can give the customer insight into your inspiration and explain how the elements of design help you express that inspiration in visual terms.

You want to share your work with others, and you want to please your audience, whether it's family, buyers at a craft show, or gallery owners and museum directors. Stay focused on what drives, inspires, and moves you. Develop ways to talk about what you do, and people will understand how committed you are to finding the best artistic solutions.

Perhaps you have doubts. What if you put your heart and soul into the work and nobody likes it? Or, what if you change from the work people have been buying and go in a different direction? You may be surprised. Often, the design that we think is unmarketable is the one that generates the most interest. And if you change your work to go to a deeper, more creative place, it is bound to resonate with people in a more profound way.

Art is a self-driven enterprise. When you tap into your deepest feelings, you are making things from an authentic place. When you are following your own curiosity, the work will ring true with others. This is work that will make people sigh with delight. This is work you can be proud of.

India. Thali marriage necklace. Gold strung on black thread. Late 19th century. Gift of Cynthia Hazen Polsky, 1991. Metropolitan Museum of Art.

PART TWO

YOUR DESIGN
TOOLBOX

This is the heart of the story: the elements and principles of design. Discover how to choose and use each of the elements to their best advantage. Think about all the different hammers there are, each one with a specific function. Have you ever wanted to make something and spent too much time using the wrong tool? Or you had a tool on your workbench and not a clue how to use it? We must understand how each element operates to achieve mastery over it. Then you will know which tool to reach for to get the desired effect.

The principles give structure to a composition. These are the concepts or themes—the big picture. For example, let's say you want to make a statement about deforestation. You're consumed with anger, frustration, and fear. You have a good idea about the lines, shapes, and textures that speak to these feelings. But how will you organize them? Consider your message in terms of balance, proportion, and contrast. The organizing principle will make your communication clear.

For every design story there are various ways to combine the elements and principles to get the job done. Your inspiration and process work together with these tools to express your point of view.

Kristina Logan. "Constellation" necklace. Flame-worked glass, cast glass, and sterling. 2011. Photo: Dean Powell.

DESIGN ELEMENTS:
The Tools of the Trade

The design elements can be roughly divided into two groups. The first group is concerned with the fundamental qualities of the parts we make. Line, shape, and form have a variety of expressive traits that we need to understand to use them appropriately. Elements are the bones of a design. Not the sexiest part of the experience, but they establish critical preliminary information. Will the piece be flat or three-dimensional? Organic or geometric? Active or passive?

If the first group of elements is the steak, the second group is the sizzle. Color, pattern, and texture are the surface treatments that bring life to the design. This is exciting stuff, but many people are intimidated by these elements. Once you know how they communicate, you will gain confidence and facility in applying them. When you incorporate them into your work, you add liveliness and personality.

The final element is position or space. This refers to how the parts of your design are arranged. It is the element that often gets overlooked, but it is essential. Choosing placement and managing negative space will make a huge difference in the quality of your designs.

Carolyn Morris Bach. "Woodland Goddess" brooch/pendant. 18 kt. and 22 kt. gold, sterling, quartz, cow bone, rosewood, and ebony. 2018. Photo: Sara Rey.

LINE

It all begins with a dot, a point in space without direction, energy, or emotion. String a bunch of dots together and you get a line. Now you've got real possibilities. The very nature of a line implies movement; it gets you from here to there. It also evokes time—that was then and this is now. You might initially think of lines as straight, even, and either vertical, horizontal, or diagonal.

Lines have three major characteristics: direction, weight, and character. When you imagine the variety of combinations of these three qualities, you realize their importance and possibilities.

Julia Turner uses line to create serious drama. The high contrast of black and white combined with the slashing crosshatched technique produces a bold, commanding surface. The three floating red lines keep this piece anchored plus add respite from the background marks. There is a sense of confusion or hostility in these lines, and placing the red lines in front gives an impression of safety by creating distance between the viewer and the turmoil.

Julia Turner. "Notation" brooch. Steel, wood, vitreous enamel, enamel paint. 2010. Artist photo.

DIRECTION

A horizontal line reads like a landscape. It is quiet, restful, and stable. A vertical line is dynamic, resists gravity, and has strength, and power, but it can also be rigid and harsh. The minute you start to move that line from upright toward the horizon, it becomes more dynamic. It picks up speed, energy, and tension. Diagonals are more exciting and have more expressive possibilities than either vertical or horizontal lines. Imagine a gently waving downhill line and compare that with a jagged zigzag at the same angle. The first is seen as a softly flowing stream, and the second as lightning. They both have more movement and personality than their straight or even counterparts. Lines that spiral or converge in the center evoke feelings of pressure and claustrophobia. These lines pull you in and make it hard to reverse direction and get free of the tensions.

WEIGHT

Wide, heavy lines have more visual weight and importance than fine, lightweight lines. Consider the bold, heavy fonts used in advertising. For example, SALE, NEW & IMPROVED, and ORIGINAL attract our attention to what's important. When combined with lighter lines, heavy lines appear to be closer to the viewer or in front of other objects. Since the heavy lines come forward and finer ones retreat, together they convey depth of surface. Lines that vary from thick to thin are evocative of contours or edges. They emphasize and describe an object. If you were to draw an apple sitting in the sun, you might draw very fine lines on the edge that's in the light, and heavy ones where the apple rests on the surface. By varying the line weight, you draw attention to or away from a particular aspect of the design.

Let's examine these two similar pieces by Donna D'Aquino and Beverly Tadeu. The formal compositions are very similar: concentric circles that describe the space and form through line only. But note the differences between the mathematical, hard-lined geometry and the organic, undulating curves. It's as if both artists were given the same puzzle to solve, and they used their unique vision and personality to find the design solution. Notice the feelings that arise from each solution. Does one feel more masculine and the other feminine? Is one more traditional and the other modern? Which one speaks to you and why?

Donna D'Aquino. "Wire Bracelet #88." Steel wire. 2005. Photo: Ralph Gabriner.

Beverly Tadeu. "Revolution" bracelet. Sterling. 2012. Photo: Hap Sakwa.

CHARACTER

The quality of a line is important in communicating a mood or idea. Wavy, curly, or undulating lines evoke natural themes. Silky hair, growing tendrils and vines, or ocean waves may come to mind when we use these lines. But what if there's a storm at sea? Suddenly you need to use different lines. Rough, jagged, and broken lines express a completely different set of emotions. Along with your storm at sea, you can picture lightning or a rugged mountain range. The energy is masculine and potent and requires using lines that express this energy. What about a chicken-scratch kind of line? It expresses anxiety, fear, confusion, and timidity, which can be used to communicate more passive emotions.

Consider these characteristics in regard to the edges of your jewelry designs as well as the individual elements. Creating a dynamic edge is a great way to add interest to a piece. Edges can be hammered, scored, painted, shined or patinated, coarsened, or refined. It's that unexpected touch that can set your work apart.

Lines can be combined to form patterns and visual texture. Stripes and plaids, cross-hatches, and squiggles can create overall surface design. Choose patterns that are in alignment with your design ideas. You wouldn't use a heavy black-and-white check pattern in a soft, floral necklace. All visual texture conveys a certain kind of energy and mood. Be conscious of what your patterns and textures are expressing.

Here is an example of line being used as surface technique. Andrea Williams has inlaid 18 kt. gold to the surface of beach stones. The lines evoke nature as they swirl delicately across the surface. There is a gentle, organic rhythm occurring between the regular pattern of the stones and the flowing surface design. Notice how powerful a design can be when the elements are limited.

Andrea Williams. "Siren Song" necklace. Beach stones, reclaimed sterling silver, and reclaimed 18 kt. gold inlay. 2016. Photo: Mark Craig.

Whether you use a line by itself or in combination with others, choose them intentionally to communicate your message and support your design. Want to create an urban impression? Choose geometric lines in grid patterns, or converging lines evoking the perspective of looking up at tall buildings or down avenues. Is your design focused on a breezy, sensuous energy? Choose gentle curves at restful angles. And if you wish to create something with a frenetic, rock-and-roll vibe, use lots of diagonals with varying line weight and character.

Use line to express your voice or style. Study the images in this book. How did these artists utilize line to convey their point of view? What thoughts and feelings do these lines express? Is this something you've been trying to communicate in your own work?

JL. Collier created these hollow-formed bangles with a whimsical feel. The fanciful edges make these pieces look fun and carefree. To help understand the emotional content of these designs, imagine what clothing you would wear them with or where you would be going when you put them on. To me, these pieces feel like a party.

JL. Collier. "Ripple, Compass Mark, and Quadra" bracelets. Hollow-formed, patinaed copper. 2011. Photo: Amy Collier.

Line Exercise:

1. Think about an activity you enjoy—as a participant or spectator. It can be anything from ballroom dancing to chess. Fill yourself with memories, thoughts, and feelings about this activity. What do you love about it? What energy does it have? What do you want to express when you tell others about it? Spend some time making random lines that express the thoughts, feelings, and energy you associate with this activity. It's not important to make an image just to play with the lines to try to express your thoughts and feelings.

2. A good way to experiment with line is to use unusual media to make marks. Gather up a variety of things you can make lines with— paint, chalk, crayons, ink, markers, etc. Think outside the box. What else can you make marks with? A branch, ribbon, fork, or sponge, and don't forget your fingers!

Now have fun. Make marks of all kinds with different emotions, energy, and pattern. Fill pages with lines and don't edit yourself. After you've exhausted all your ideas, lay the work out and examine it. Are there lines you prefer and others that turn you off? Can you imagine using some of these lines in your current work? Where are the surprises?

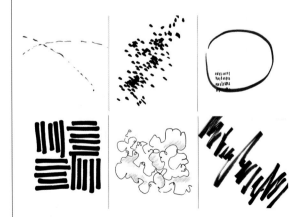

SHAPE

A shape is created when lines enclose space. The lines form the boundary, and a shape is what we call the space inside the lines. It is two-dimensional—it has length and width and comes in two varieties, geometric and organic.

Geometric shapes are precise and mathematical. They include squares, circles, triangles, ovals, and rectangles. Geometric shapes are stable, regular, and easily incorporated into jewelry designs because they are balanced and orderly. These shapes are so universal and versatile that jewelry makers have used them across cultures and throughout history. A quick perusal of jewelry designs anywhere will illustrate this point. Circles are represented in beaded necklaces, ovals and triangles are found in pendants and earrings, and rectangles are used in every kind of jewelry component. Basic geometric shapes give you a frame for all kinds of surface design. They can also be an innocuous background to which the viewer pays little attention, because all the interest is on top of this shape.

Stretch a basic geometric shape and you generate more energy and dynamism. A stocky triangle will become an arrow pointing powerfully with fierce energy. A circle turns into a long oval or teardrop, whose gravitational pull gives it more weight and more emotional possibilities. Don't shy away from geometric shapes because you think they are traditional. See what you can do to make them more dynamic and modern. Instead of focusing on their static nature, emphasize their universality.

Organic shapes are subdivided into three types: representational, evocative, and abstract. These shapes are derived from nature, so they don't follow the strict rules of geometry. A representational shape is a likeness of something in the natural world, from the human form to clouds and everything large, small, or in between. It can be used as iconography or part of a narrative. This is one way to create very personal design that is easily understood by the viewer.

Take a representational shape and abstract it a bit and you produce something evocative. You create a shape that is easily understood as a leaf or a star, for example, but is not a true likeness. Evocative shapes have more freedom and personality than representative ones. They can be stretched or truncated to suit the situation. Salvador Dalí showed us clocks that were melting. They didn't look like real clocks, but we understood what they were. Use evocative shapes to create fantastical designs and for more personal expression. Some artists are so strongly associated with a certain kind of shape that it becomes part of their voice.

The red necklace by Kat Cole has a very modern attitude. What do you see in this piece? It could be a deconstructed cityscape or the furniture and appliances in your home—sink, stovetop, tables, and even the front door! It could be a political statement about the waste our culture generates. However you interpret it, there is a sense of the manufactured, urban environment and the decay that occurs with time. The shapes and negative space are provocative and keep your eye moving around the piece, finding new tidbits of interest along the way.

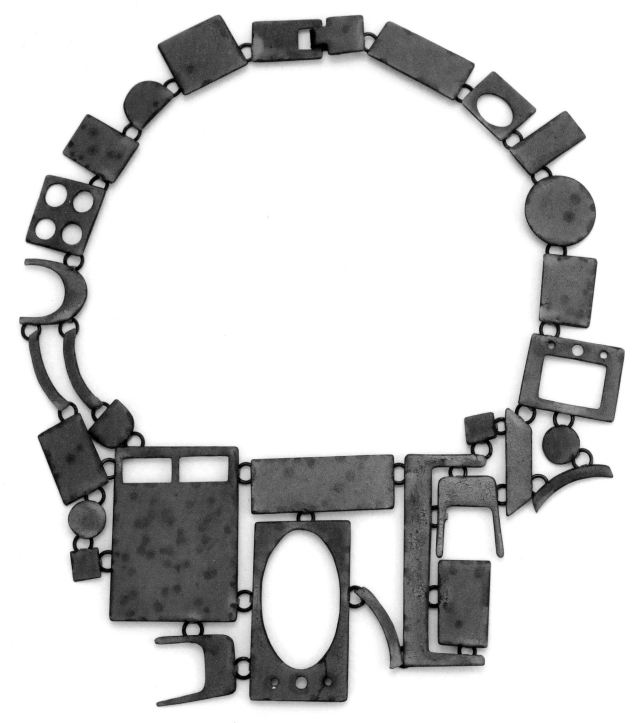

Kat Cole. "405 Summit Catalog of Belongings" necklace.
Steel, enamel. 2012. Artist photo.

The necklace by Jane Adam is an example of evocative shape. These undulating shapes might be petals, leaves, or seashells, but they definitely depict natural objects. The feminine sensuality and overall lushness in this piece are not bound to the subject matter. Using a vague shape such as this allows for a broader appeal. The viewer can make their own associations, come to their own conclusions, and appreciate it for their own reasons.

Jane Adam. "Ochre Pearl" necklace. Dyed aluminum, freshwater pearls, oxidized silver. 2018. Photo: Joël Degen.

If you release all semblance of figurative likeness, you have total abstraction. These shapes are random and can be whatever the artist needs in a specific situation. Think of creating shapes that express the feeling you get while listening to your favorite music. What would a jazz-inspired design look like? How would it differ from one influenced by pop music? What kinds of shapes would be kindled by your favorite meal? Or your favorite pastime? What shapes would you choose if inspired by a season?

It isn't just geometric shapes that express tradition. Organic shapes can evoke a historical place and time. Traditional symbols such as the fleur de lis, yin yang, the hamsa, and celtic knots, for example. The lazy snake shapes of art nouveau, the fans and fronds of art deco, the highly stylized midcentury motifs, and the funky florals and paisleys of the 1960s are all examples of traditional organic shapes.

Angela Bubash uses one simple shape, the oval, changing the size and articulation of the element to create movement, variety, and playfulness. There is a sense of joie de vivre but something else as well. As the oval plates head this way and that, there is a notion of change, flux, and agitation. Shadows grow and shrink as light conditions change, and there's a shift of color as if from full light to deep shadow.

Angela Bubash. "Fin#30" brooch. Sterling silver, glass, feathers. 2011. Photo: Mary Vogel.

Here is the important part. Shapes are critical because they are often the first impression you have of a piece of jewelry. They are what you see at a glance or from a distance. They can affect the design in subtle or substantive ways. The shapes you choose must be in alignment with the message you wish to communicate. Squares and rectangles express all things man-made: buildings, books, furniture, picture frames, and more. Objects that are solid, structural, and precise. A circle is the universal symbol for wholeness, the infinite, planets, and community. Its universality makes it an excellent choice for a wide variety of jewelry designs. Most of us feel a connection to circles. Each shape has its own place and time.

Different types of shapes express different ideas and feelings. If you are inspired by music or the rhythm of the tides, by sunrise or deep woods, leave geometry behind. If you have a story to tell, use representational shapes as symbols or iconography. And if you want to convey formal compositional ideas, choose either geometric or abstract shapes. Choose consciously and your communication will be clear and sharp.

Whatever you are designing, remember to rely on your process. Identify the kinds of shapes that work best with your theme or message. Create lots of variations of these initial ideas, as discussed in the section on inspiration. Then begin to narrow your focus by analyzing each version. It will quickly become obvious that some options are better left for another time. Choose a few to go forward with, and refine these ideas. The ultimate question is "Do these shapes support my theme or do they detract from it?"

Once you've selected the shapes for the current project, arrange them in different configurations. This will create new shapes from the spaces between and around the components. These new shapes are called negative space. Negative space can be more easily understood by picturing a person standing with hands on hips. The human form is the positive shape or space, and all the shapes around the body and inside the bent arms are the negative space. Interesting negative space is crucial to good design. Whether you are making a brooch, a necklace, or earrings, consider how it will look on the backdrop of the body and visualize the negative space around the jewelry. Can you make it more interesting by moving elements around? Does the outline or negative space align with your theme or inspiration?

By now you're getting the idea that *all* aspects of design need to be considered at all times. Don't worry. Remembering all this information can be challenging at first, but in time it becomes second nature, and you will be amazed at the tools you have to solve your design dilemmas.

When it comes to figurative, representational shapes, here is a wonderful example by Michael Romanik. This design illustrates a striking use of shape repetition. The shape of the wren with its distinctive erect tail is mimicked by the overall shape of the composition. The ovoid leaf shapes are repeated in the bird's wing and on its chest. And the side-by-side branching pattern of the leaves is echoed in the tail feathers. The patterning brings to mind the decorative arts of the past: ancient Egypt, Asia, and Mesoamerica. The intentional choices produce a clear and concise design story.

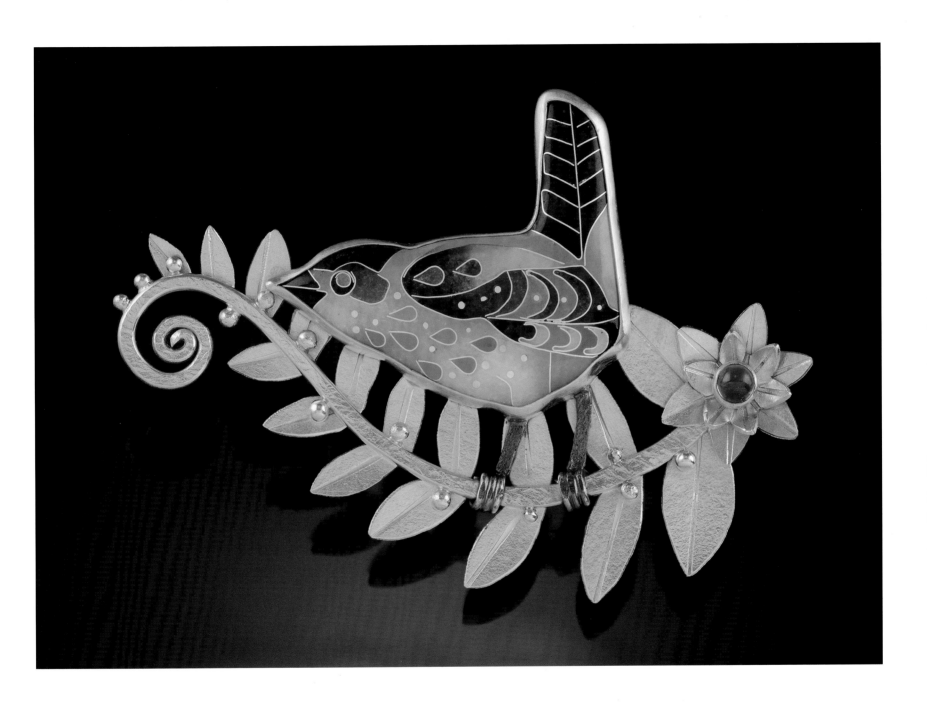

Michael Romanik. "House Wren" brooch. Cloisonné enamel, fine silver, sterling silver, and blue topaz. 2010. Photo: Larry Sanders.

Shape Exercise:

1. Geometric shapes—choose two or three shapes and create some designs using drawing materials, paper cutouts, Colorforms®, drawing apps; whatever suits you. See how interesting you can make them. Don't edit yourself at first. Just make a bunch of them.

2. Different configurations—varying the size, number, balance, and articulation. Only limit the number of shapes. Now analyze what you've done. Which designs speak to you? How can you make things more dynamic? Do you envision rings, pendants, brooches?

3. Organic shapes—do the same exercise with organic shapes. This time, however, think about expressing some emotional content: joy, safety, worry, fear, pressure, tenderness, etc. Think of a time when you had a heightened emotional experience. Really put yourself into the memory. Now imagine how you might express that with shapes. Once again, make a bunch of these without editing yourself. Save the analysis for later. Get the feelings flowing through you and into your designs. Now can you use these ideas in your jewelry design? Does is fit with what you're currently working on or does it give you ideas of what to do next?

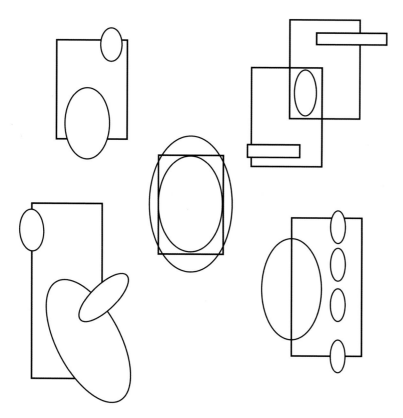

This brooch by Lauren Pollaro is an example of abstract composition. The rough, rocklike shapes are used to move your eye around the design. Notice how the directional length of each element acts as a pointer for your gaze. Their position creates balance; the largest element is equalized by the negative space in the bottom right. The design is unified by the surface decoration: the repetition of rivets, the colors, and textures. A formal abstract design doesn't require that you find meaning in the piece. You might notice references to landscapes or architecture, but these are incidental. The movement and balance make this design complete.

Lauren Pollaro. Brooch/pendant. Vitreous enamel on copper, sterling silver, brass, gold fill, altered canvas, thread, gold leaf, and found object. 2017. Photo: Charley Frieberg.

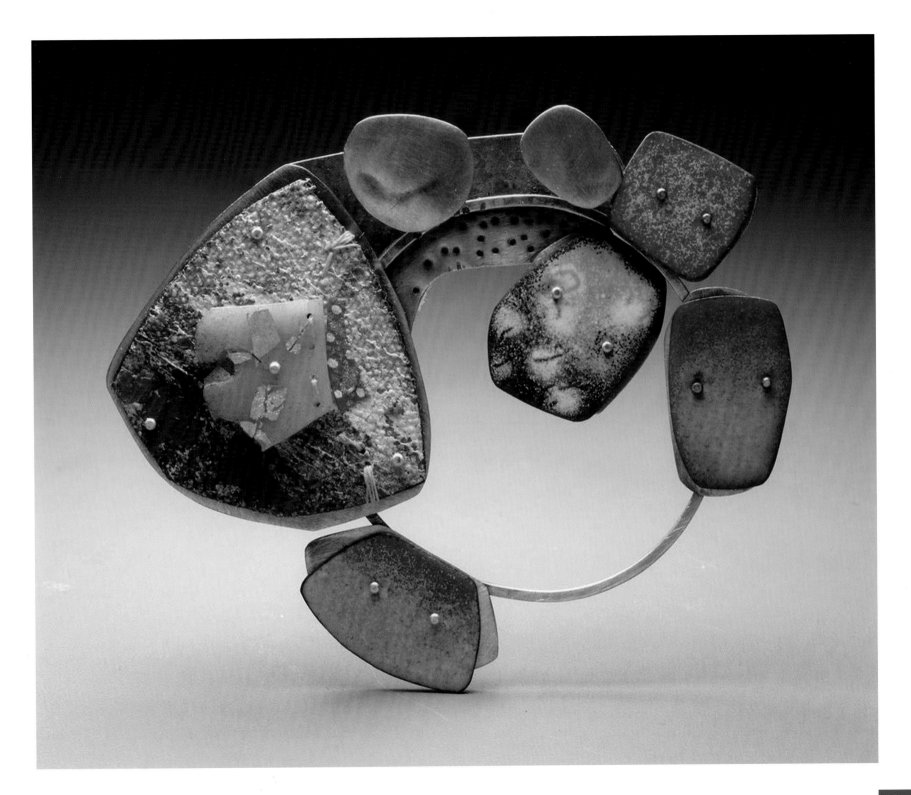

FORM

Forms are three-dimensional shapes. They have length, width, and depth. The third dimension gives them weight or mass, which adds to their dynamism and potential as design elements. Forms can be geometric or organic, representational or abstract.

Geometric forms correspond to geometric shapes. By adding the third dimension, squares, circles, and triangles become cubes, spheres, and cones, for example. A geometric form is a mathematical or regular object that is precise in all its angles and edges.

Organic forms are irregular, often asymmetrical, and more dynamic. They represent nature, as animal or plant life. They also represent abstract concepts, emotions, and ideas. Their main qualities are undulating line and unconstrained movement in space. They are not restricted by the mathematical qualities that keep geometric forms grounded.

These brooches by Regine Schwarzer are excellent examples of the skillful use of geometric, three-dimensional forms. There is universality in this design, which allows us to experience them from our own point of view. Do they look like a jumble of rocks on the seashore, a crystal formation, or maybe a bunch of empty packing boxes? You can write your own story with these pieces. Your eye travels effortlessly around the composition, watching the play of light and shadow and the dance of positive and negative space. The visual interest is remarkable considering there is essentially one simple geometric form.

Regine Schwarzer. "Isometric Formations" brooches. Sterling silver, coral. 2009. Photo: Michael Haines.

Melanie West takes us on a visual adventure with this large, hollow-formed cuff bracelet. The curves swell and contract with a slow and sensual rhythm. The attitude is hedonic and blowsy, and it makes you want to touch it. The colors match the overall mood, and the scale of the patterns supports the easy tone. Everything works together to sustain the artist's intention.

Melanie West. Bangle. Hollow-formed polymer. 2018. Artist photo.

The ring by Dominque Audette is a wonderful example of symmetrical, organic form. Although it is an abstract, formal composition, there is a sense of mosques or minarets from exotic lands. Every twist and turn in this design supports the others, creating a sense of unity in the whole. This piece does what great art should do—it takes you away from your daily experience and transports you to another reality. One of the artist's imagining, which exists in a private dialogue between the viewer and the piece.

Compare the mood or attitude with this ring by Philip Sajet. One evokes the romance of exotic lands, while the other is contemporary and chic. Notice the unique balance achieved when the focal element is shifted to the edge of the band. Everything about this design pushes the limits of standard ring design. The thick, heavy band and the stark, dense, diamond-shaped solitaire complement the bold, simple design. It demonstrates unity and high contrast at the same time.

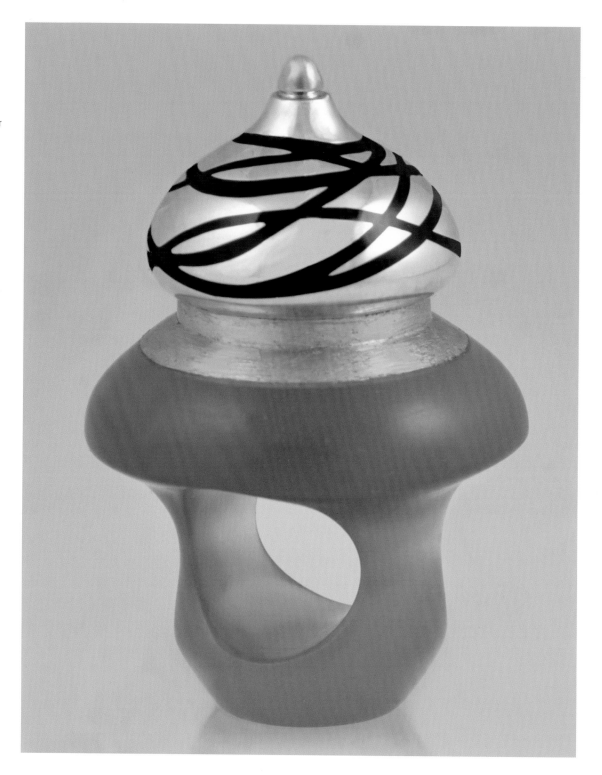

Dominque Audette. "Istanbul" ring. Sterling silver, 14 kt. gold, 24 kt. gold leaf, resin. 2013. Photo: Etienne Beland.

Forms can be used alone or clustered together; for example, one single ball as an earring, or a group of balls gathered into a brooch or necklace. Forms can be open or closed. A closed form is a solid, opaque mass. If space exists within the form, it is contained and confined. An open form reveals its structure and therefore has a more fluid and dynamic relationship with the space around it. A ribbon twirling through midair is an example of an open form. The form consists of the ribbon plus the space in and around it.

Because it is three-dimensional, a form is meant to be viewed from all sides, like a free-standing sculpture. Shapes having only two dimensions are viewed from one direction, like a painting.

In two-dimensional design the artist is concerned with organizing the picture plane in interesting ways, moving the eye around the composition, creating balance, flow, and unity, etc., all within the two-dimensional plane. Sculpture must consider all these things in 360 degrees. In a drawing, you can approximate the space and weight of the objects pictured through light and shadow. But in a sculpture, the parts take up actual physical space. The artist must consider how the parts communicate with each other and how the viewer perceives them. When you add mass to your jewelry elements, the compositional possibilities multiply.

Philip Sajet. "On the Edge" ring. Cut and polished river stone, niello on silver. 2018. Artist photo.

Regarding jewelry design, both two- and three-dimensional issues are in play. Often jewelry pieces lie flat on the body and are viewed from one direction. In this case, the artist approaches the design with two-dimensional considerations. Just as often we see earrings, rings, and some bracelets that stand away from the body and are viewed in the round. They require a more three-dimensional approach. Jewelry design is unique in this respect. It requires the artist to consider both 2-D and 3-D design issues. Most jewelry, however, is a hybrid, flat-backed with three-dimensional parts and pieces, like a low-relief sculpture on a building's facade. This is what makes jewelry design unique: the fact that considerations of both flat design and design in the round must be part of the process. When you hear a certain piece of jewelry referred to as sculptural or painterly, this is what they mean.

Which is your preferred style—flat shapes or forms in the round? Perhaps there are more possibilities for your work on the horizon. By incorporating new shape and form ideas, you may find a whole new path. Be sure to choose shapes and forms that best communicate your ideas.

The necklace by Jeffrey Lloyd Dever exemplifies the negative-space possibilities of form. The eye is drawn to the outside edge of each dangling pod. There is a rhythmic undulation as your vision moves from left to right, disturbed only when you reach the focal element. Here the artist slows our attention and invites us to take a closer look at the finer details. The repetition of the pointed forms and polka dots in the stamens and pistils creates a back-and-forth tension. The vibrant color enhances the composition and adds another level of interest and sophistication. Taken as a whole, your eye is as interested in the objects as it is in the space around and between them. This is masterful control of form and space.

Form Exercise

The only way to experiment with form is to work three dimensionally.

Take some modeling clay and experiment with creating different types of forms: static, dynamic, open, closed, fluid, and geometric. Look at the forms you create under a single-sourced light. Study the structure from all sides. It's helpful if you have a turntable. Notice how the play of light and shadow affects the form. This is a fantastic exercise for people who design mostly through drawings. Doing things differently usually has a stimulating effect on our work.

I suggest using polymer clay for this exercise. It is readily available, easy to work with, firm enough to keep its form while you work with it, and cures in a home oven, so you can keep your design experiments.

Jeffrey Lloyd Dever. "October's Blush" necklace. Polymer clay, nylon-coated steel cable, anodized niobium cable, lacquer. 2011. Photo: Gregory R. Staley.

Color

Color is arguably the broadest and deepest subject in art. There are enough books written about color to make it a lifelong study. Color theory encompasses a multitude of concepts, definitions, and applications—enough to fill your bookshelves. We can't cover it all—but you will get enough information to more confidently use color in your design process. There is some technical information that you need to know. Plus, understanding the emotional and psychological effects of color will help you communicate more effectively. Finally, there is the power of palette building: putting together the best color combinations to express your ideas. This is the fun stuff! Color has energy, creates a mood, evokes memories, and brings the flavor. Color is very personal and one of the best ways to express your unique point of view. Successful use of color is more about expressing emotion than it is about color theory. Let's start with some fundamentals.

When light hits an object it is either absorbed or reflected. The reflected light waves bounce back to us in varying proportions, and this is what we perceive as color. The earliest references to color theory go back to the fifteenth century. Leonardo da Vinci and other Renaissance artists were interested in color mixing and the emotional effects of color in their work. Two hundred years later, Sir Isaac Newton expanded the theory through his work with prisms. He invented the first color wheel and gave us the rainbow colors that children still memorize today—red, orange, yellow, green, blue, indigo, and violet. From Newton to today, color theory has grown, morphed, and progressed. It's an exciting and complex topic, but for successful jewelry design we need to understand the broader concepts.

The first characteristic of color is hue. This is the defining attribute of the color. Hue is what we *call* the color; for example, pink or gold or lime green. Primary colors are the hues that cannot be reduced. All other colors are mixed from the primaries, which include red, yellow, and blue. When two primary colors are mixed together you get a secondary color. These are orange, green, and violet. Tertiary colors are the result of mixing a primary with a secondary. For example, red plus orange will yield an orangey red or vermillion. The color wheel gives you a snapshot of where the colors are in relation to each other. For example, you can see that blue and violet combine to make plum.

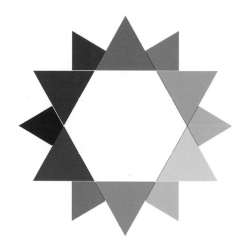

We have strong feelings about color, both positive and negative reactions, especially when it comes to what we wear. This enameled brooch by Kaori Juzu shows the subtlety and sophistication of a toned-down palette. The shapes and colors evoke a rocky coastline. The enamels feel like the rocks are partially wet, as if splashed by a wave. The color scheme is complementary, yellow and violet, but the low value makes the color more natural and cohesive and reduces the contrast.

Kaori Juzu. "Dances at Dawn" brooch. Enamel, copper, silver, 14 kt. gold. 2010. Danish Craftsman Prize. Collection of Designmuseum, Denmark. Artist photo.

Anarina Anar has a facility with color. This palette is called a split complement. Instead of choosing just two opposite colors, the artist has chosen four: blue and turquoise from the cool side of the color wheel, and red and orange from the warm side. The mastery here comes in establishing a color hierarchy. Using equal amounts of warm and cool would set up a static situation. In this design, blue and turquoise are dominant. The warm colors play their part, bringing energy and excitement to the piece. They keep the cool palette from feeling heavy or sad. And the touch of yellow green adds pop to the design.

Anarina Anar. "Blue Splash" necklace. Polymer and copper wire. 2018. Artist photo.

Colors opposite each other on the wheel are called complementary colors. Those on either side of a hue are called analogous. Complementary color schemes yield a dynamic interaction with lots of drama and sparkle. For example, notice that orange and blue are opposite each other and therefore complementary. An orange-and-blue color scheme might include the darker and lighter versions of orange and blue. The tints and tones will help keep things from being overly bright and reduce the vibration.

Analogous palettes are harmonious and compatible but have low contrast and energy. An analogous color scheme could include red violet, violet, blue violet, and blue. This would be a soft, sensual, and calming palette. However, choosing the pure hues from the color wheel is not the most interesting way for colors to interact.

Value will enrich your palette. Value refers to how light or dark a color is. Think of it as a gradient scale from white to black, with progressively darker grays along the path. Adding white to your hue results in a tint. Add black and you get a shade. If you mix gray with your hue, you get a tone. Adding tints, tones, and shades to your color work brings it into the realm of natural color with all its variety. This is how we actually perceive color in the world, with highlights, lowlights, and shadows. Include the hue you started with, also called the native color, and an object in natural lighting has four distinct values. Without the value scale, colors are pure and

bright but also flat. They compete for attention. It's like an elementary school recital, with each child singing at the top of his lungs to be heard. It is the addition of value that creates three-dimensionality. Take some time to experiment with value; start by choosing one color that you like. Mix white into that color a little at a time until it's almost pure white. Then, starting with the initial color again, mix a little black into it until it's almost black. You will quickly see the possibilities for more interesting and complex color.

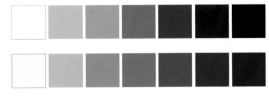

The third characteristic of color is intensity or saturation. This refers to the relative amount of pure hue there is in the color. Is the color full strength or diluted? An intensity scale starts with pure straight-from-the-tube color. Then add gray, a little at a time, until the color is almost pure gray. Intensity is also referred to as the brightness of the color. This is a little misleading—a pure yellow is much brighter than a pure violet. The practical need for understanding hue saturation is in color mixing. If you know the color is pure hue, you have a better idea of how much black or white is needed to create tints and shades. If a color is too bright or strong, tone it down by adding either its complement or gray. If all your colors have the same intensity, the effect is modern, graphic, and flat. If you want a more natural, dimensional quality in your color work, make sure to include a range of value and saturation.

Color temperature refers to our perception of the relative warmth or coolness of a color. Red, orange, and yellow are said to be warm. They remind us of fire and sunlight. Warm colors appear more active and advance toward us. Blue, green, and violet are the cool colors, like the sky, water, and trees. Cool colors seem to recede and are passive. But each primary color has a warm and a cool version. Why is this important? There are two reasons. First, pure, warm colors have greater vibration when placed side by side. Colors with a strong vibration can be difficult to look at. A cool green next to a toned-down red will produce less contrast and bounce. Second, color temperature helps us improve our color mixing. When two colors have the same temperature, the newly mixed color will be clear and bright. But if you mix warm and cool colors together, the result is earthier tones. Neither is right or wrong; it all depends on what you are hoping to express with color.

There are no good or bad colors. There are only good or bad color relationships. Our experience of color is dependent on light and the neighboring colors. Just for a minute, cover up the yellow triad in the above figure with a piece of white paper. Suddenly the bottom red and blue adjacent to the yellows look richer. Take the paper away and watch them change back. It is your job to set up good color neighborhoods and to build more dynamic relationships.

This is analogous color. The bracelets by Meghan O'Rourke explore the possibilities of warm and cool palettes. But the two palettes elicit very different feelings. How do you interpret these color stories? In each case, the petal shapes create a lovely rhythm like leaves rippling in the wind. Compare the soft, gentle color of these bracelets with the intense colors in the brooch by Isabelle Carpentier.

This analogous scheme starts with yellow and yellow green and moves into green and blue green. The color is rich and bold. The limited palette works well with the tightly packed pattern. There is highly restrained energy in this piece, as if the bundle could break apart at any moment. The energy is supported by the color, texture, size, and radial symmetry. Is it imploding or about to explode?

Isabelle Carpentier. "La Broche Verte" brooch. Brass, glass paste, steel, and gold mosaic. 2018. Photo: IC Atelier.

Opposite: Meghan O'Rourke. "Unfolded" bracelets. Titanium, sterling silver, 18 kt. gold. 2007. Photo: Grant Hancock.

Color has a profound physiological effect on us even though we may not be conscious of it. Every day our emotions, moods, mental acuity, and even physical sensations, such as appetite, are influenced by the colors that surround us. Color can affect our perception of temperature, and the weight or size of objects. It can raise or lower blood pressure, heart rate, and the performance of the endocrine system. Advertisers and interior designers rely on this information to affect our purchasing habits.

The psychological effects of color are diverse. A particular color's cultural significance can vary markedly. For example, in many Eastern cultures white is the color of mourning, while in the West it's bridal. Of course, there are also personal reactions to specific colors. Some colors we love and others we avoid. The way you use color will become part of your personal style. Consider your relationship with color and how you use it to express your individuality. Most of us know the colors we are attracted to. Look around your home, your garden, or your wardrobe. You will find clues about your relationship with color. Do you prefer bright, clear colors or rich jewel tones? Are you more comfortable with natural color combinations or does neon color turn you on? Getting in touch with your unique color personality will transform your art.

Now that you understand how color works and how it affects us, you can make intentional choices. Choose colors that calm or excite you or make you gasp or sigh. Use color to harmonize and unify a design. Or do the opposite and create contrast. Color can set a visual path and generate movement or produce pattern and rhythm. Use color to create emphasis and establish balance. The skillful use of color is one of the most important and versatile design tools at your disposal. The time you spend increasing your understanding and facility with color will reap benefits in your art.

Rebecca Hannon has a contemporary approach to complementary color. By choosing orange red and blue green as her complements, she has reduced the contrast enough so the colors are lively but don't vibrate. Adding the pale gray–blue also grounds the palette and keeps the intensity in check. Notice the grayish edges of these shapes. This is another way to maintain control of the bright complements. The stunning color combined with the movement of the shapes establishes a sparkling pattern and rhythm. It shows how unity and variety can be used in the same composition very effectively.

Rebecca Hannon. "Crown of Thorns" neckpiece. Laser-cut laminate, slotted together. 2015. Photo: Jacob Mailman.

WHAT DO YOU WANT YOUR COLOR TO DO?

Create unity or harmony: Use shades of one hue or analogous colors.

Create atmosphere: Use lights, darks, and tertiary colors for a natural effect.

Create contrast or energy: Use highly saturated or complementary colors.

Create pattern or rhythm: Repeat colors at prescribed intervals.

Evoke temperature: Establish a warm or cool palette.

Effective color palettes should include darks and lights, dulls and brights. This is how we perceive the world around us: highlights, lowlights, local color, deep shade, and a touch of the unexpected. Even in a black-and-white composition, use this concept to enrich the visual experience. Purposefully use black and white to create a mood, and enhance it by introducing the gray scale. In your metalwork, mixing surface finishes from high shine to patinas will set up a gray scale that will produce visual depth and create atmosphere.

How do you put all this together? Hue, intensity, value, and color relationships—there's so much to consider. The solution is design dominance. When you're in the kitchen making soup, you follow a recipe that tells you how much of each ingredient to add to the pot. You know you need a lot more protein than salt, for example. If everything went into the soup pot in the same quantity, dinner would be a fiasco. This concept is at the heart of design. You need to establish a hierarchy that is strong and clear. I suggest proportions of 60-30-10 percent as a loose rule of thumb. Your principal color gets 60 percent of the design space. The supporting colors get about 30 percent, and the accent colors—the spices—get 10 percent. This is a basic strategy. Very quickly, you will integrate the concept and start pushing these proportions to come up with more sophisticated color stories. Setting limitations on your work will reduce the feeling that there are too many choices, and allow you to delve deeper and come up with more creative solutions. Without limits your color work will look haphazard. You'll be more successful with a concept and a plan.

Color Exercise:

1. Spend time actively looking at color. Even when you observe an all-green landscape, look closely to take in the variety of greens. There are warm and cool shades, and light, dark, and muted colors too. Notice how they create unity, harmony, and variety. All the essential elements are present. Look at paintings and study their color schemes. Or floral design, fashion, or advertising. When you come across a palette that makes your scalp tingle, photograph it, write it down, sketch it, or rip the page from the magazine. Somehow take those colors with you, because this is where you live on the color wheel.

2. Think about something you believe in—your philosophy, motto, or creed. Something you hold dear. Let yourself get into it; experience the passion you have for this ideal. Make a list of words that describe what it means to you. Make the list emotional and intimate. Choose colors that fit the words, emotions, and concept. Add the types of lines, shapes, patterns, and textures to illustrate the words. Now that you have the parts—start building a design.

Creating Effective Palettes

Shaping a purposeful palette is the way we express moods or emotions. There's no definitive right or wrong; the goal is to build a palette that feels a certain way to you. Let yourself go, express yourself, and release those preset ideas about what color "should" look like. Here are several ways that will help you become more confident with color.

1. Visit the paint department at the hardware store. Here you can pick up hundreds of colors to play with. At home, cut them into squares and start to pick out the ones you love. Choose about a dozen and put the rest aside. Analyze what you have. Do they remind you of something or somewhere? What feelings come up from these colors? Are there colors that don't fit in? Or maybe you have two batches of color. Does it feel like something is missing? Adjust the selection until you love the combinations. Glue the chips into your sketchbook and write down the words or phrases you think the colors express.

2. Monochromatic color scheme uses tints, tones, and shades within the same hue or color family. Choosing a color that you love, create

lighter and darker versions of it. Also include bright and dull versions of the color. These colors will inherently go together because they are all versions of the initial color. Monochromatic schemes are safe and easy to control and sometimes have an old-fashioned look, like sepia print photos.

3. Complementary color schemes use colors that are opposite each other on the color wheel. Perhaps a red violet and yellow green. As pure hues, these colors have a lot of contrast, creating too much vibration. So choose one of them to dominate the palette; the other will have a supporting role. Use darks, lights and tones of each to help them harmonize.

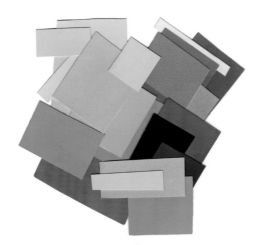

4. Analogous color schemes use three or four colors that are side by side on the color wheel. Yellow, yellow green, green, and blue green, for example. Depending on which slice of the color pie you choose, you will get different moods or feelings. This yellowy-green section of the wheel makes me think of spring, youth, freshness, hope, and maybe tenderness.

Choose the blue through violet part of the wheel and you might get feelings of nighttime, coldness, serenity, or luxury.

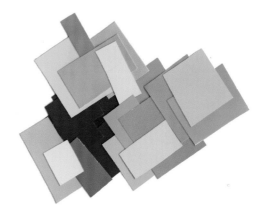

5. Find the colors that fit your mood by starting with a list of words that express the thoughts, feelings, or states of being that interest you. For instance: dynamism, nostalgia, dreaminess, youth, modernity, primitivism, magnetism, grace, urbanity, joy, comfort, spirituality, or opulence. After you choose a word, start building your palette with the colors that come to mind. Use the word as a beacon. Measure the colors against it. Do they express that idea to you? Play and experiment until you find the right combinations and that feeling shines through.

PATTERN

Pattern illustrates how the principles and elements of art work together to create a composition. Pattern is the repetition of elements in a consistent, regular manner. Rhythm is the overarching plan to create a tempo through the repetition of regulated elements. In other words, pattern is the tool you can use to create rhythm. For each principle, there are elements that will get the job done and others you may wish to avoid. But pattern and rhythm go together like a hand in a glove.

As surface decoration, stripes, dots, and repeated motifs can be carved, painted, hammered, or etched onto your piece. Patterns are created directly in your medium as a surface treatment or applied to the surface with pigments or veneers. Pattern also refers to the repetition of a shape or form. In any case, it is the regular arrangement and repetition of elements that creates the patterns and subsequently the rhythm.

The first thing that comes to mind when we talk about pattern is some fabricated or manufactured object. Polka dots or checked fabric, stacks of cups at a coffee bar, or the girders of a suspension bridge. These man-made patterns are generally geometric and have metered uniformity, which is a 1-1-1-1 count. This is the simplest form of rhythm and not very exciting. Varying this simple pattern will add appeal and flavor to your work.

Patterns exist in nature as well as in manufactured objects, and it is useful to compare the two. We find patterns in every form of nature, from microscopic life to the cosmos, although recognizing patterns in nature can take deeper analysis and consideration. Think about the growth rings of trees, the seed pattern in the center of a sunflower, or the stripes on a zebra. There is the regularity in both man-made and organic patterning. Patterns are organic or geometric, regular or irregular, structural or decorative, positive or negative, and repeating or random. Which kind of patterning appeals to you?

The "City Necklace" by Daphne Krinos illustrates the excitement potential from alternating patterns. There is the long and short play of the architectural shapes. The lighted windows create a second layer of pattern that is more random. And a third, less obvious pattern consists of flat shapes and three-dimensional forms. Although this design consists of simple rectangles and a one-color contrast, we recognize that it's a cityscape. The palette encourages us to see it as a city at night. The effect is so complete that you can almost hear honking horns and people calling for a cab!

Daphne Krinos. "City Necklace." Ruthenium-plated 18 kt. white gold and white diamonds. 2017. Photo: Sylvain Deleu.

TYPES OF PATTERN

Rows exist when stripes or other
    elements are arranged in lines.

Grids alternate a pattern both horizon-
    tally and vertically, like a
    chessboard.

Alternating patterns are offset from row
    to row, like brickwork or tiles.

Half-drop patterns alternate like
    brickwork but add a space between
    rows. Honeycombs and leopards'
    spots are examples of half-drop
    patterning.

Radial patterns are found in snowflakes,
    flower petals, and mandalas.

Spirals are seen in galaxies, seashells,
    and the fiddleheads of ferns.

Branching is a common form of pattern-
    ing in the plant world. Tree
    branches and roots come to mind,
    but also river deltas, ice crystals,
    and lightning.

Packing refers to the ways in which
    compacted cells define each other's
    shape, as in a cluster of soap
    bubbles or a colony of mushrooms.

Cracking is the break-up patterning seen
    in the dried surface of mud or old
    paint, as well as tree bark, animal
    hides, and rock formations.

Nina Morrow uses two kinds of pattern in this driftwood necklace. There are the repeated wooden sticks nestled together in a crisscross, back-and-forth, regular beat. The black dots randomly dance across the surface, leading us around the necklace. The alternating patterns create an easygoing, playful rhythm that makes this necklace one you might choose for a party. The decision not to use a clasp helps reinforce unity in the piece. There is no break in the rhythm and no end to the fun!

Nina Morrow. "Natural Stick Collar with Dots" necklace. Driftwood and elastic. 2015. Photo: Margot Geist.

Ruth Ball plays with surface pattern on these enameled pendants. There are repeated motifs, gentle arcs, dashes, and wavy lines, which create staccato rhythms. The artist breaks up the surface with color, wire, and gold leaf, creating a strong sense of layering and depth of surface. The color is pretty and delicate. The resulting design is modern, hopeful, and fresh.

Ruth Ball. "Winter Landscapes" pendants. Vitreous enamel on copper, sterling, silver cloisonné wire, and gold foil. 2008. Artist photo.

Patterns can be used alone or in combinations. The successful mixing of patterns, like other aspects of design, requires that you set up a hierarchy, selecting a principal pattern and its supporting cast. Assign each pattern a scale—small, medium, or large. Depending on your concept, one of these sizes will seem best suited to dominate the current design. For example, if you want to make a bold, powerful statement, choose large patterns. Give the principal pattern the most space. The other sizes will support and enhance the main pattern by being subordinate to it.

Without a distinct hierarchy, your design suffers. Choose only large patterns and the effect is overbearing, like someone shouting. Too many small patterns and the piece feels fussy, and if all the patterns are medium sized, the design will be boring. Finally, if you choose equal amounts of several patterns, you will produce a static, flag-like quality devoid of any highs and lows. Remember that no matter how much surface decoration you add, it's a good idea to leave some space in the design for the eye to rest and the mind to reflect.

This enameled brooch by Danielle Embry is an example of packing. The repeated cup forms make me think of lichen. The clustering is exactly how these plants occur in nature. The organic pattern, soft color, and undulating shapes combine to set a mood that is calm and dreamy. Although the piece is evocative of a natural scene, it is ambiguous enough that we can infer different things. Where I see deciduous woodland, you may see coral or barnacles. This elusive meaning gives the work a broad appeal.

Danielle Embry. "Peeled" brooch. Enamel on copper, sterling silver. 2010. Artist photo.

With all this information about patterning fresh in your mind, go exploring. Notice the different kinds of patterns on view in your environment. Look for both man-made and natural examples. Also, look through your jewelry books for examples of how artists use different types of pattern. How do you respond to them? Did you find a favorite? How will you incorporate these ideas into your own work?

Stephan Hampala employs two kinds of pattern in this necklace. The bead forms themselves are a regular pattern. All the same size and shape, they march around in a circle to a 1, 1, 1 beat. Second, there's the surface pattern of the beads. Each has a unique geometric design, with a common texture and muted palette. The soft gray, gold, and copper keep the geometry from feeling cold or calculated. Instead, this piece has a cozy feel, like a favorite sweater.

Pattern Exercise:

1. Draw variations of the patterns discussed above. Try them all: rows, grids, alternating and half drop, radial, branching, packing, and cracking. There's more to patterns than stripes and dots!

2. Use your printer or tracing paper to make several copies of one of your pieces of jewelry. Examine the basic shapes without all of the ornamentation. Now imagine the kinds of patterns that might enhance the piece. Try several different ideas on the copies. What happens to your design? How much pattern should you add—a little or a lot? Does adding pattern change the energy and emotion of the piece? Is it a change for the better? Make sure the feeling of the pattern complements the mood of the piece.

Stephan Hampala. Necklace. Antique glass beads, wooden
spheres, oxidized silver. 2005. Photo: Peter Volker.

Texture

Texture is the perceived tactile quality of an object's surface. There are two types of texture: physical and visual. Physical texture refers to the actual feel of an object. It can be rough, slick, bumpy, jagged, soft, gritty, or smooth. The textures can be created either by removing some of the surface, by adding to it, or by the inherent feel of the materials. Fibers, beads, and natural or found objects all have inherent physical textures. Artists are often drawn to a particular medium because of the textural qualities. We just love the way it feels, and spend precious time and effort to enhance the touch of the finished work.

Visual texture is what photographs and certain paintings rely on. It is the illusion that within the two-dimensional surface, the objects have texture. In jewelry design this illusion is created with color, pattern, and transparency. A smooth surface can have the appearance of roughness, or a flat surface can appear to have depth. Patterns make elements come forward or retreat and create vibration or the illusion of space. Using such materials as glass, resin, and polymer, artists can build layers of physical texture trapped under a smooth, transparent surface. This creates an enticing illusion of depth.

Andrea Gutierrez's linen cuff has an abundance of textures, colors, and patterns. The artist sets up an underlying repetition of pattern with silk circles in several sizes. This moves our gaze over the surface of the piece. She adds beads here and there—large and small, round and faceted. The variety of elements holds our interest. A third layer of bead clusters and stacked groups give the piece richness and depth of surface. The artist selected each element to create a luxurious tactile experience. Like a decadent bubble bath with candlelight and champagne, the effect is feminine and extravagant.

Andrea Gutierrez. "Unbridled" cuff. Beads: gold vermeil, sterling, citrine, aquamarine, tourmaline, garnets, vintage glass, Thai silver, moonstone, peridot, topaz, amethyst, ruby, carnelian, antique metal seed beads, steel cuts and round, embroidered on silk, cotton, gold, and silver metallic threads and a cast sterling silver clasp. 2016. Photo: Elio Tolot.

In fact, texture can become the subject of the design. You can develop rhythm with texture. Or use texture to build unity, create movement, and support balance. A small, highly textured area draws attention and creates emphasis. Develop contrast by playing passive areas against active textures. This versatile element can help reinforce any principle you choose.

Texture adds emotion, energy, and individuality when used purposefully. Rough, deep textures have more visual weight. They reflect light dramatically, adding contrast and energy. Smooth, shiny surfaces reflect light evenly and draw our attention. We equate shine with cleanliness, newness, and modernity. If this is what you are interested in, then slick, shiny surfaces would be your choice. Matte surfaces reflect soft, diffuse light and create atmosphere and mood. They look touchable, warm, and inviting.

What emotion and energy come to mind when you envision the following textures: velvet, tree bark, eggshells, glass, or mushrooms? What texture is your hair or the shirt you have on? Everything has texture, and we associate a time, place, and feeling with most of them. Use your memories, thoughts, and personal associations to choose textures for your work.

Some contemporary jewelry has the look of an ancient artifact made by primitive hands. The work of Enric Majoral seems even older, as if formed at the dawn of time by climactic geologic events. It feels like it is of the earth and not made by an artist's hand at all. This is an interpretation of the form, but mostly the effect of the texture. It makes a powerful statement—no flourishes needed.

Enric Majoral. "Joies de Sorra [Sand Jewels]" ring. Sterling silver and acrylic paint. 2007. Photo: Majoral.com.

Everything in your field of vision has texture. Everything you touch and everything that touches you has texture. What would life be without the sense of touch? Touch is an enjoyable sense, and we are fortunate that jewelry invites people to actively use this sense. It adds another level of engagement, allowing the viewer to experience the art more fully. It is highly satisfying when people pick up your work and caress it. Their sense of enjoyment is palpable.

Using texture can increase interest in a composition by adding variety without changing other relationships. Collect textures for engraving, etching, and stamping; for mold making; or simply as inspiration. Gather up unusual materials with interesting textures to incorporate in future designs. Accrue a cache of tools for texturing: hammers and engraving tools, chisels, linoleum cutters, or gouging tools. My texture box has everything from seashells to burlap and other cool stuff.

Nature inspires artists in many different ways. Cycles of life and death are potent in Anna Johnson's hand. The artist strives to rouse us to the interconnectedness of the world we live in. There is sensitivity and tenderness in the imagery, which is enhanced by colors and textures. Imagine if the hibiscus pod were cast in silver. The feeling would change dramatically from warm to cool. A strong underlying geometry keeps us focused on the subject and organizes the various elements. This allows a moment to think about life, loss, and dignity.

Anna Johnson. "Syriacus" brooch. Grossular garnet, rainbow moonstone, bat skull, fine and sterling silver, cast bronze hibiscus pods. 2015. Photo: Steve Mann.

Jed Green's work illustrates the tantalizing quality of visual texture. There is a lot of variety and action inside these beads. My fingers fairly itch with a desire to hold this piece. In the hand the experience would be slick and smooth, with the exception of a few matte elements. The repetition of circles as surface design and within the focal bead produces a unified whole, making a unified statement. To ensure unity, the artist reduces the palette to a value scale, from frosty white to black. The work is powerful, modern, and a riot of fabulous textures.

Mix and match textures in a hierarchical way. Vary the amount of different textures. Keep one prominent and let the others take the back seat. Texture can add flavor, but it should always support the overall design plan. Be conscious of how the textures work together. There is a time for clashing energy and another for harmony. Choose carefully.

Consider layering your surface design. Color, pattern, and texture can work together as they do in fashion and interior design. Imagine one overall texture in different colors or patterns. Or select one color in a variety of textures and patterns. There are endless possibilities for creating a rich, tactile surface that invites touch. Establish the major strokes and secondary aspects and then add pops of contrast.

Remember that your goal is expressing ideas, emotions, or philosophy to your audience. Art communicates your worldview, without words, through the use of the principles and elements of design. The principles set the agenda for the design. From line to texture, the elements have distinct characteristics that combine to make a statement. Whether you are interested in balance or rhythm, movement or variety, unity or scale, choose the principles and use the elements to support them. In the end, your design will speak for you.

Jed Green. "Cluster Necklace." Glass, paint, silver, wood, freshwater pearls. 2017. Photo: Tas Kyprianou.

In a painstaking process called micromosaics, Cynthia Toops lays down tiny polymer threads to create the image within the silver bezel. There is one simple texture—a thin strand of polymer in different colors and lengths. The excitement is created by the narrative. This is the story of a contented gardener caring for beautiful plants on a sunny day. All this is accomplished with one textural element. Imagine telling this story in one color or with one type of line. Can you envision how different the result would be?

Cynthia Toops. "Garden Series #3" brooch. Polymer threads, sterling bezel by Chuck Domitrovich. 2000. Photo: Roger Schreiber.

Texture Exercise:

Take a texture walk with your camera. Make a long list of texture words and go out looking for them. Snap pictures at random of all the items on your list. Are you finding new textures? Analyze this "texture catalog" for future use in your jewelry designs.

POSITION

Space and position are concerned with the areas around and within your design. Space can be positive or negative, open or closed, shallow or deep, two-dimensional or three-dimensional. In two-dimensional art there are many ways to give the illusion of space, depending on the position you choose within the picture plane. With three-dimensional art, position refers to points on an object, while space refers to the actual space an object occupies.

It's an old adage that the three most important things in real estate are location, location, location. This applies to design as well. Where you put an element within a composition drives the effect that element has on the design. Whatever it is, it will have greater or lesser impact depending on where it settles.

Lin Stanionis is the master of her design elements. This design starts off with a very potent, symmetrical center piece—it's practically a target. A circle with a hole in the center has incredibly strong visual pull, but the artist doesn't want our attention to get stuck there. The floral elements create a triangular shape that supports the circle, and the branches move the eye from point to point. These strong points of interest make the entire design one you will spend a lot of time analyzing and enjoying. Putting the snake head at the bottom of the focal piece keeps the eye moving and leads us down to the bottom of the composition. It's interesting that an organic design has such a strong underlying geometry. You might try using a geometric framework on which to build your design.

Lin Stanionis. "Awakening" brooch. 18 kt. gold, sterling, garnets, enamel, snake skeleton. 2013. Photo: Jon Blumb.

In Western art, the traditional tenet is that we read a design space as an interior or a landscape. We visually "enter" the space at the bottom left and work our way up through the design, exiting somewhere near the top right corner. In Asian art, paintings are viewed vertically, with the eye bouncing back and forth along a central line, top to bottom or bottom to top. In modern culture our visual set point has been affected by graphic design, from advertising to web design. We enter the design space near the center, and there we find the cues about where to look next.

Elements placed high in the visual field are seen as active, important, and dynamic, while elements near the bottom feel stable, heavy, passive, and grounded. The visual center is the strongest, most stable position. The farther away from the center you go, the stronger the dynamic pull of the element. This can create an additional nexus of interest, or it can pull too hard and break the cohesiveness of the design.

Jewelry design is a little different. You may not be trying to give the illusion of depth, but if you understand how to manipulate the elements by the position they are in, you will be able to more effectively communicate your ideas.

The strong graphic look of Allison Hilton Jones's brooch is a superb illustration of how position is critical. Imagine you are redesigning this piece. What would happen if you moved the orange balls down to the equator? What if they came out the top of the donut form? Neither of these solutions would be effective. The power of this piece comes from the placement of the elements, the negative space, and the interaction of materials. This is very smart design.

Allison Hilton Jones. "3 Lines 2 Balls" brooch. Sterling silver, concrete, and felt. 2016. Photo: Cole Rodger.

Position can be used both to separate and connect elements in a design. Wider spaces separate elements from each other, and smaller spaces connect elements to create groupings or bigger parts. Overlapping shapes or forms maximizes their relationship. The form on top is closer to the viewer, increasing its importance and potency.

Value, size, color, and texture can all be used in the same manner to establish significance and order. If you want an element to appear closer or have a more powerful role in the composition, you can increase the value contrast, make it brighter or bigger, or give it coarser texture. Conversely, if you want the shape or form to have less importance or seem farther away, make it smaller, duller, with lower contrast, or with finer texture.

How do you decide where to place these greater and lesser parts? That depends on your intention. Dead center is the most potent spot in the visual field. It draws the viewer's attention and holds it there. For this reason, it is commonly and traditionally used in necklace, earring, brooch, and ring design. Sometimes it is used to establish symmetry, starting in the center and moving out at regular intervals. It is common for an entire design to be based on the focal element: a gemstone, found object, or enameled piece, for example. The surrounding components are simply there to point to or show off the focal piece. Obviously, when your eye isn't roaming around the design, looking at other curious bits, you spend more time contemplating the focal element. However, dead center is static and has such a strong pull that it's hard to shift the viewer's attention to other parts of the design.

If you want a bit more energy and dynamism, choose a focal area that's off-center. Many contemporary jewelers choose a spot that is just above and to the right of the visual center. This position has many of the same characteristics as the center: strength, impact,

Let's examine this ring by Monique Rancourt. What do you think about the placement of the white topaz? Can you picture it in another spot? Would it have the same impact? How about the dark tubes? They draw our attention and move the eye around the design, but what if they were clustered together on one side? Or surrounding the stone? Or clustered in the center? Notice the outside edge of the design—the negative space creates significant movement in the piece. All the decisions about placement have been made to create a dynamic visual experience for the viewer. Imagine the possibilities in your work.

Monique Rancourt. "Crustacean Ring." Cast sterling, white topaz. 2010. Artist photo.

and stability. But it has more energy and allows for more interesting spatial relationships and movement. As you push design elements toward the edges, you create a more dynamic and stimulating design space that will sustain the viewer's interest.

Take a moment during the design process to focus on the negative space. By shaping the negative as well as positive space, you create rhythm, unity, and movement. Imagine music with no space between notes. All the notes played together, by all the instruments, at the same time. The music disappears and it's just noise. Without space between the notes, we lose all comprehension. The same is true with visual expression. Well-controlled negative space improves your communication by creating a hierarchy with areas of emphasis

and areas of rest. The negative space allows the viewer a moment to let the design information sink in and be appreciated. Without space, all you have is noise.

Clustering like elements creates a strong sense of unity. Spreading them around creates movement, rhythm, and harmonies. Using overlap or changes in size, color, shape, pattern, or texture creates interest, balance, and dynamism. If you want to make a quiet, serene, and stable piece, keep your focus central, with dominant elements low in the design space. Keep your negative space fairly uniform and passive. If you want a more dynamic design, move the energizing elements around the design. Add the color, texture, or form away from the center and keep the viewer's gaze active.

How can you use position to convey a variety of meanings? Imagine how you would use design elements to express the following conditions: luxury, solitude, claustrophobia, calmness, excitement, distance, cuddling, drama, purity, and strength. What kind of lines, shapes, color, textures, and patterns would you use? And how would you organize the design space?

Andra Lupu uses overlap to expand the illusion of depth in her work and then flattens it out by making all the elements in one size, shape, and material. The piece gives the impression of falling leaves or petals, and the haphazard way the shapes overlap feels natural and organic. The negative space is effectively handled. It moves our eye in and around the piece with the help of some dramatic shadow play. Because of position, the negative space is not just the outside edge but includes the edges of all the shapes

Andra Lupu. "Crushed Collection" brooch. Sterling, stainless steel. 2016. Artist photo.

Chris Carpenter uses symmetry in a modern context. The tourmalines are strong, vertical elements that set up the symmetry. The circles reinforce the balance with their left-to-right equilibrium. But notice where the circles are located vertically. They are not centered under the stones. If they were, the design would be static. The little gold balls at the edges imply a gentle spinning motion. Combine that motion with the crucial placement of the gemstones on the discs, and you have a modern symmetry that is compelling and smart.

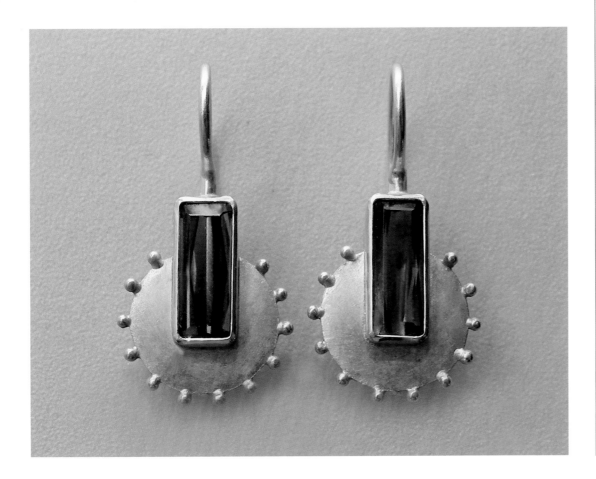

Chris Carpenter. Earrings. 22 kt. gold, tourmalines. 2015.
Artist photo.

Position Exercise:

Use your Colorforms® or shape cutouts or a drawing app.

Use only one color and one shape. This helps minimize the variables so you can really see the effect of position on the design.

Create a design. Then move one element at a time to see how things change.

Record your variations by snapping a photo, using tracing paper, or saving variations digitally.

Compare versions to see how position affects the composition.

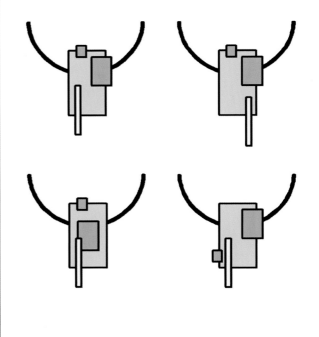

DESIGN PRINCIPLES:
The Overarching Concepts

Design principles are the concepts or themes used to organize the elements. They are the purpose or main point of each composition. They act as the North Star to guide your design decisions. With each choice, ask yourself, "Does this get me closer to or further away from my goal?"

The three cardinal principles are unity, movement, and balance. All successful design employs these three. They are the foundation of our creative endeavors: unity is the sense of wholeness created from the various parts, movement directs the viewer's gaze to all aspects of the composition, and balance is the visual equilibrium that enhances the harmony in each design. These principles establish a foundation for the composition. When these principles are present, the work is intentional and the message is clear; without them the design looks haphazard or confused.

The remaining principles are a smorgasbord of design options. Are you interested in the drama of contrast or the subtleties of rhythm? Do you want to excite the audience with issues of scale or thrill them with variety? Perhaps you have a fascination for focal points. Discover all the ways to create emphasis, and follow that path through experimentation and play. The choice is yours and will be easy to make when you understand which principles align most closely with your vision.

UNITY

The principles of art are the overarching concepts that govern how we organize design elements. Unity and harmony are the most fundamental of all the principles. Unity occurs when all the elements work together to create a balanced, complete whole. Harmony is when the elements create a pleasing visual experience. Without unity, the design will be chaotic. Too much similarity of elements makes the work bland so that it doesn't hold our interest. Too much diversity and it can be hard to look at.

Unity is the lighthouse that guides your selection of elements. It's about telling one story, serving one master plan, expressing one point of view. Unity gives the artwork a sense of cohesion and coherence.

Unity is instinctively recognized as the sum of the compositional elements. It is the gestalt of seeing the whole before the individual parts. It holds the design together both visually and conceptually. With unity, the elements do not compete for attention. They work together to express the message. The design is viewed as a pleasing unit and not a collection of parts. It emphasizes your concept or theme and communicates your thoughts and feelings.

Harmony is the pleasing arrangement of components. It engages the viewer and creates an inner sense of order and beauty. Harmonious elements have a logical relationship to each other; they go together in an expected way. Like a choral group with all the members singing their parts, the result is harmony. It's the big, cohesive sound we experience before hearing individual singers.

Bruce Metcalf. "La Petit Mort" brooch. Carved and painted maple, Micarta, gold-plated brass, sterling, glass cabochon. 2015. Artist photo.

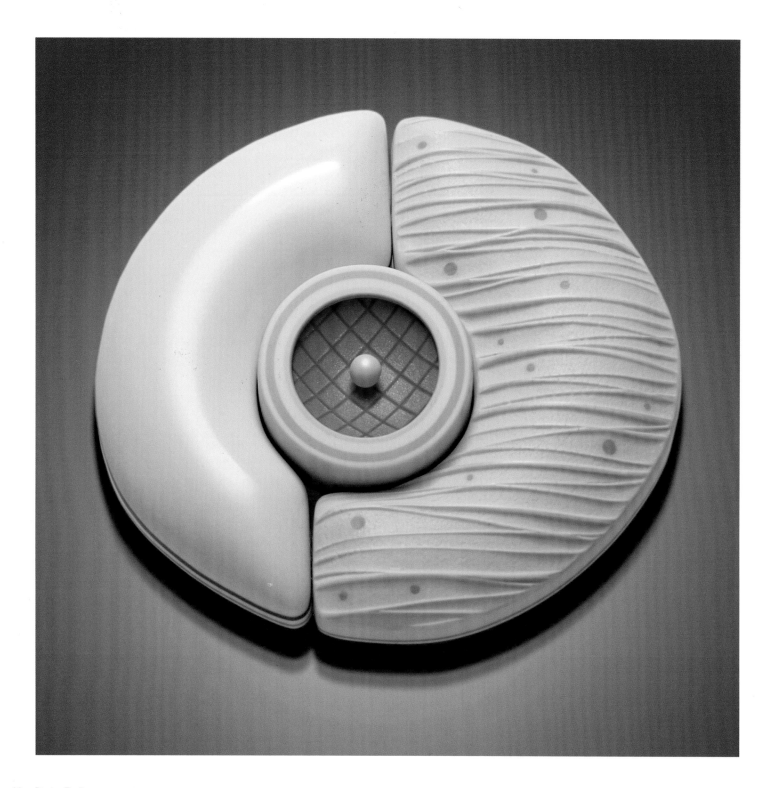

Everything about this brooch by Dan Cormier is cohesive: the way the forms nestle together and merge into a new form. The reduced palette: white and shades of gray with a muted orange for interest. The repetition of linear and circular elements; the dots on the right side echo the ball in the center. The contrast between the precise, geometric center and the organic outer form, plus the strict orange grid against the white, organic, crisscrossed lines. All the elements are harmonious, complementary, and soothing.

Carla Pennie McBride tells a similar story in this metal-and-resin brooch. Notice the parallels: the overall circular design with a just off-center focal area; the repetition of lines and dots; the subtle interest at the edges and the reduced palette. There is a lot of correlation, but you would never think these two pieces came from the same artist! This is the magic of art. Two artists from different parts of the globe, telling comparable stories, in different media, and in their own unique voices. Universality and individuality travel hand in hand.

Above: Carla Pennie McBride. "Swirl Pin." Sterling and fine silver and epoxy resin. 2010. Photo: Blair Clark.

Opposite: Dan Cormier. "Polar Pin." Polymer clay and steel wire. 2009. Artist photo.

Ashley Buchanan's "Chaos Chain" is anything but chaotic in my view. The artist has successfully utilized simplicity, similarity, and repetition to unify her design. One basic element repeated in various ways. Flat chain, block chain, or lacy-cut work are literally linked together. The finishing flourish is the brilliant yellow powder coat, which provides a fresh punch of energy.

There are two kinds of unity to choose from. *Visual unity* refers to having all the design elements align to create one visual experience. Select the line, form, motif, and texture that have the same energy or tone. Then arrange these components to create consistency. *Conceptual unity* is merging the physical forms and the meaning of the piece to create the whole. It's about the narrative. The parts combine to tell a specific story. If you want to depict abundance, for instance, you would choose motifs that symbolize abundance, affluence, profusion, or opulence to you and reinforce the message with rich colors and ample shapes. To me, abundance evokes the harvest time, with ripened fruits and vegetables bursting with goodness. Translating that idea into a piece of jewelry, I would choose voluptuous, rounded forms and luscious, deep colors. In both types of unity, choose elements that support each other and work together to create the whole. Avoid mixed messages. Select elements that belong together and the message will be clear.

Ashley Buchanan. "Chaos Chain" necklace. Hand-cut brass, powder coat. 2016. Photo: Joshua Dudley Greer.

Wendy McAllister's use of one color and one shape creates unity in this piece. There's one clear message. What's interesting to me is how she keeps the piece vibrant and lively within the unified arrangement. There is still movement and balance in this homogenous design. By changing the size and articulation of the shapes, each little bloom has its own identity. It's like the choir all warmed up and singing one note.

Wendy McAllister. "Blue Hydra" brooch. Vitreous enamel, copper, and sterling. 2011. Photo: Hap Sakwa.

Here are specific ways to create unity in your jewelry designs:

SIMILARITY

Items with similar or identical characteristics such as size, shape, color, or texture will be perceived as a group by the viewer. Like a sports team whose players all wear the same uniform, we see the group and not the individual players. Scattering similar elements throughout the piece will also help pull the composition together.

SIMPLICITY

Like similarity, harmony can be achieved by keeping things simple. Restrict your color choices, choose one overall texture or pattern, or have all the elements move in one direction. Keep the variety to a minimum. Your aim is to produce one rounded, whole sound, so limit anything that is different.

REPETITION

Repeating elements such as shapes, lines, or motifs in a regular and predictable way will produce harmony and unity. Things that look alike appear related to each other. Using repetition creates a bond between the parts, and the design fuses into completeness.

PROXIMITY

Objects that are close to each other appear to be related. Place elements next to or on top of each other, and the brain melds them into one larger form. Whatever combines parts to forge a new, bigger element in the viewer's mind or eye creates unity.

ALIGNMENT

Like proximity, you can produce unity by placing elements along a common axis. It's the connective tissue that makes them appear more related. Like piano keys or brussels sprouts on the stalk, the alignment makes the connection in our brains.

CONTRAST

Remember to add just a little contrast. A little variety within the design will keep things fresh.

These are the unifying factors. The goal of your design is to communicate a cohesive message, one clear idea or emotion. The more unified the elements are, the more distinct your message will be. We are naturally attracted to wholeness; it gives us a sense of well-being. Completeness is calming and emotionally satisfying. Communicate this feeling in your designs, and your viewer will sigh with contentment.

Unity Exercise:

Try using the various methods to create unity in your designs. Similarity, simplicity, repetition, proximity, alignment, and contrast. Is there one way you enjoy most? Did you have a difficult time working with any of them? Analyze some of your finished jewelry pieces. How much of a part does unity play in your work? Is there anyplace it is missing?

Gustav Reyes bends wood. He honors his source material by creating elegant, wearable jewelry. Here he uses one continuous piece of cherry, which swirls around itself in a grand, rhythmic gesture. There are no breaks in the continuity and no extraneous information. Just one clear swoop of a message.

Gustav Reyes. "Greater Than" bracelet. Steam-bent cherry wood. 2010. Artist photo.

MOVEMENT

The goal of jewelry design is to communicate ideas, arouse emotions, pique curiosity, and connect with your audience. You must keep the viewer engaged in the work. Movement creates a visual path that directs the viewer's attention into and around a composition. Without movement, the design becomes stagnant, boring, or obvious. If the viewer is able to instantly absorb the design, they will surely move on to something more compelling. To keep people engaged, the artist must tell a story or take us on a journey. Movement directs us to observe, wonder, and feel what the maker intended.

The first step in creating movement is to decide what's important about the piece, and to choose the elements that best support those ideas. As you work through the design process, keep that objective in mind.

Visual movement can be achieved in a variety of ways: through the use of gestural and directional lines, repetition, position and size of objects, color, shape, and form, as well as the relative position of these elements.

LINE

Movement can be directed along lines, edges, and patterns. By its very nature a line is a path. It represents time and space and therefore movement, especially when it is a diagonal, a zigzag, or an undulating curve. Our gaze naturally follows the line. By strategically choosing lines, you can gently influence the viewer's attention. Construct a path through the design by repeating patterns, textures, shapes, or motifs, directing the view to the important parts of the composition.

SHAPE

Unless you choose circles or squares, all shapes have a specific directional tendency. The longer dimension leads the way. Stretch the shape or form and the gaze will follow that direction until another significant element stops or redirects it. This is called continuance. With continuance, small cues link together to create the visual path.

However, these directional cues can lead the viewer right out of a composition. This may not be desirable; it certainly wouldn't be in a painting or sculpture. But jewelry design has the advantage of the intimate relationship with the human form. A dominant element may lead the attention out of the piece and onto the arm, for example, and, thanks to continuance, right back into the design. This creates a grand gesture and results in highly dramatic work.

There are strong directional cues in these earrings by Petra Class. The geometric shapes have a stepping-stone effect. The shapes create a visual rhythm, undulating in and out in a lazy figure eight. All the hard edges and stone facets are softened as the brain blends them into an organic form. The small variation in the direction of some stones doesn't detract from the design; instead it effectively adds contrast.

Petra Class. "Green Mosaic Earrings." Tourmaline, emerald, and 18/22 kt. gold. 2009. Photo: Hap Sakwa.

Paulette Werger shows us how one element can engage the viewer when movement is employed. The artist uses simple curved lines, stacks them up, and shuffles them around, all the time controlling the negative and positive space and . . . voilà! The artist has created an interesting design that holds our attention. There are so many relationships and areas to explore. The story is organic but also architectural, simple, and complex and evokes feelings and memories.

Paulette Werger. "Scattered Bundle" brooch. Fabricated, and fused and oxidized Argentium silver. 2016. Photo: Charley Freiberg.

Try placing your design elements in various positions and angles. Create an underlying geometry—a figure eight, a triangle, or an S curve, for example. Then position the components along this underlying structure. Reposition the parts until you get the movement you want. Each compositional area or element should direct the eye to another area. But be careful to avoid setting up a "black hole," which draws the viewer in and arrests the visual flow, dominating the composition.

COLOR

Warm colors generally appear closer and more active than cool colors. We are attracted to warmer colors; they grab our attention, as do shiny textures and anomalous forms. Use these elements as contrast and elicit the visual pop of excitement that catches the eye and holds the attention. The repetition and rhythmic use of color are an enjoyable way to control the movement. We find ourselves looking around for our favorite color, like following a trail of bread crumbs.

CLOSURE

Our brains like to fill in the blanks and complete partially seen things. This helps us make sense of the visual world. Small parts group together, to be seen as a larger form, or dotted lines become complete shapes. Leaving a little something to the imagination can create a more rewarding experience. We enjoy working out some of the details for ourselves.

VISUAL RHYTHM

Our brains like to have paths to follow. Rows of windows, birds in flight, and intricate tile patterns—there is rhythm in our daily life, and our vision follows happily along. Visual rhythm establishes movement in your work and generates a mood and a feeling, just like musical rhythm does.

PROXIMITY AND ALIGNMENT

Elements that are close together or aligned with one another will be combined into a bigger form by our brain. Overlapping shapes or forms, adjacent textures, or patterns that repeat will come together and coalesce into something more. This grouping of close or aligned elements is another way our brains reconcile the visual world.

Bonnie Bishoff and J. M. Syron use a variety of elements to get our attention and keep us engaged. The tumbling shapes might be the first thing you notice. They generate visual cues that tell us where to look next. Then there's the color and pattern. My eye is drawn to the orange shapes, and my gaze bounces around the piece until there are no more orange areas to discover, and then it moves on to green. But you might prefer the magenta and yellow. In any case, the movement delightfully holds our interest.

Tia Kramer uses many of the same techniques in her necklace but achieves a very different effect. By using rich, deep colors and rectilinear shapes, the artist has set a more intellectual tone. Take a moment to compare and contrast these pieces. Make a list with "Bishoff" on one side and "Kramer" on the other. Write down the specific elements each uses to create movement in their necklace. Note the reactions you have to each piece. What ideas, feelings, or memories do they evoke? Which piece do you want to touch or wear? This is a good exercise to hone your analytical skills and test your design knowledge.

Top: Bonnie Bishoff and J. M. Syron. "Autumn Zephyr" necklace. Polymer with millefiori marquetry, stainless-steel wire, and sterling clasp. 2015. Photo: Dean Powell.

Bottom: Tia Kramer. "Fluttering Series II" necklace with detachable earrings. Sterling silver and handmade paper. 2011. Photo: Hank Drew.

Movement is never boring. It adds excitement, drama, and interest to jewelry design. When you direct the eye you generate action and give the viewer a richer experience than if they take in all the visual information at once. Let the elements in your composition create movement and a path of discovery.

All of this directing the viewer's attention may sound like manipulation. It is. But not in the same way that advertising manipulates us. Our artistic intent is to express ideas and feelings. We want the audience to see things the way we see them and to feel a personal connection to the work. Movement leads the way.

Here's an example of how movement plays off the human form. The herbaceous shapes twist and turn and climb up the arm as they crawl down the hand in this cuff by Cheryl Eve Acosta. The curved lines lead out of the piece, onto the body, around the wrist, and back again to the bracelet, making good use of the environment in which we view the piece. This is a technique specific to jewelry design. Very smart!

Cheryl Eve Acosta. "Convergence" bracelet. Oxidized copper. 2010. Photo: Gene Starr.

Movement Exercise:
Go back through the images in this book or examine other jewelry pieces you love. Can you identify the visual path? What techniques or elements are used to influence your gaze? Had you noticed this before? What would happen if you added these techniques to your work?

BALANCE

Nothing that we see is perceived in isolation. We see things through a psychological lens. Nothing is really black or white. Everything is colored by our dynamic experience of it. Balance is the perception of equilibrium, and that perception depends on our association with the object we're looking at. Our eyes and brains conspire to give all objects meaning on the basis of their location, size, shape, and brightness, and our association to it. Design elements work to establish energy and tension in a composition. Our job as artists is to find the most pleasing arrangement to equalize the perceived weight of unlike parts. Easy, right? Let's see how it's done.

We talk about balance in relation to a central axis or point in the composition. This is not a geometric reference. You are not trying to figure out where the mathematical center is. Once again, it is the perception of equilibrium, so it is the perceived center of gravity, pivot point, medial axis.

This gorgeous necklace by John Moore illustrates symmetry. But it is a slightly modified symmetry. The diamonds are scattered in a roughly symmetrical way, their randomness bringing more life to the design. There is enough symmetry that the piece feels balanced and stable, and enough variety to feel fresh, elegant, and stylish. An exact mathematical arrangement would make this design feel fussy and pedantic. A little variety can have a huge impact.

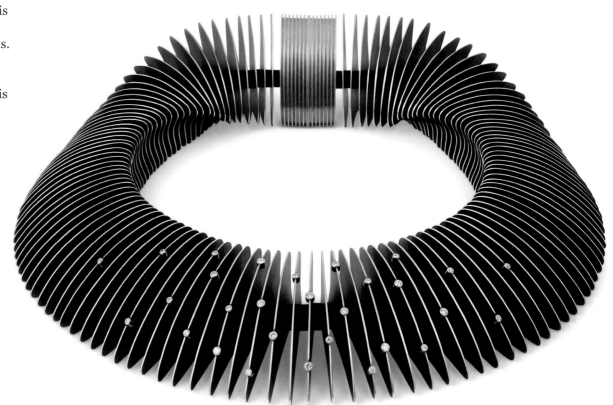

John Moore. "Silver and Diamond Verto Necklace." Sterling silver, 18 kt. gold, 29 diamonds, magnets, silicone, and steel. 2015. Artist photo.

TYPES OF BALANCE

SYMMETRY

This form of balance is achieved by locating identical compositional units on either side of a vertical or horizontal axis. When equal elements are arranged in the same manner on both sides, like a mirror image, the result is bilateral symmetry or formal balance. Symmetry conveys a sense of order, rationality, and permanence. It is easy to look at, comfortable, stable, and restful. Women like symmetrical jewelry. It is effortless to wear and makes for pleasing accessories, because our bodies are essentially symmetrical. A symmetrical necklace or pair of earrings enhance the wearer's features and give her the feeling of completing an outfit.

Keep your ideas fresh and contemporary. Symmetry doesn't mean boring or old-fashioned. Deliberate choices will make your symmetrical designs exciting and new.

MODIFIED SYMMETRY

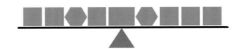

This is a variation of symmetrical balance in which equivalent but not identical elements are arranged across the axis. Also called approximate symmetry, this type of balance allows the artist some latitude in their choices. Without repeating identical units, you can easily insert subtle variations that produce more satisfying tensions, visual dynamics, and interesting relationships. This is a very popular choice for jewelry makers. It maintains the stability and order of bilateral symmetry but with added personality or spice.

Do you see this pendant as symmetrical or asymmetrical? There is a virtual line running right down the center, enhanced by the pattern within the stones. That's symmetry. But then the artist plays around with the directional framing components, moving the eye this way and that, creating interest and dynamism, and yes, asymmetry! Elaine Rader does an excellent job with the big-three principles. This piece has unity, movement, and balance.

Elaine Rader. "Golden Triangles" pendant. Sterling silver, 22 kt. gold, reticulated silver elements, opalite, ocean jasper, agate drusy. 2018. Photo: Ryder Gledhill.

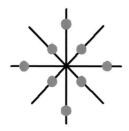

Another variation of symmetrical balance, in which the elements are arranged equally around a central point, as in the spokes of a wheel or the ripples on a pond when a stone is dropped. Radial symmetry has the strongest focal emphasis since the design is organized around a central point. Radial balance has such a potent gravitational pull that the smallest variation draws attention and adds interest. Picture a snowflake, a daisy, or a mandala. These are examples of radial symmetry. Have you ever tried building a design around this principle? The result is a strong sense of unity but an equally important need for variety.

Judith Kinghorn has a way with radial symmetry. The petals, stamens, and center ruffles are radially arranged in this wonderful "Spoonflower" brooch. Everything is balanced around a central point, which is obscured by the ruffle. This was a smart decision because it reduces the strong pull of the center, which otherwise could keep us from seeing the rest of the composition. In fact, all her elements are slightly off. The design is organic, not geometric, and that's just what the subject matter calls for.

Judith Kinghorn. "Spoonflower" brooch. 24 kt. and 22 kt. gold, sterling silver. 2015. Photo: Dani Holzschuh.

ASYMMETRY

This is where things get interesting. How do we create the perception of equilibrium when using disparate components? The visual units on either side of the axis must be carefully arranged to create the sense of balance. Obviously, asymmetrical or informal balance is more complex and difficult to achieve. It takes knowledge and skill to harmoniously balance objects of varying visual weight. But when you accomplish it, asymmetrical balance brings more variety, interest, and dynamism to your work. It heightens the emotional impact and dramatic tension. You may find it challenging, but asymmetry results in unique and highly personal work. Remember, while symmetry first establishes unity and then adds variety, asymmetry chooses variety and then works to balance the disparate elements.

DISCORDANT OR OFF-BALANCE

There is a time and place for breaking the rules, but it must be purposely done. Why would you want to create an off-balance design? Perhaps to arrest the viewer's attention, provoke ideas, or push the envelope. It may be fun to experiment with designs that are off-balance, but remember, this is not an excuse for poorly conceived or executed work. It must be an intentional choice to make a specific point.

This fanciful neckpiece by Lora Nikolova brings to mind the paintings of Joan Miró. The primary blue and red and the high contrast of black and white give us so much to look at. The directional lines lead the gaze around the piece in a lyrical singsong rhythm. The artist locates the largest elements near the center to control the balance. Imagine you are dividing the image into four quadrants. Notice that they are fairly equal in weight, importance, and activity. This is a check for balance. This artist enjoys asymmetry, which makes our interaction with her work enjoyable too.

Lora Nikolova. "Abstract Neckpiece." Glass, resin, semiprecious stones, ceramic, resin, and tiger tail–covered steel wire. 2016. Artist photo.

Achieve balance by engaging the elements in the following ways:

Line:

Thick lines have more weight than thin lines. Jagged or rough lines have more weight than smooth or straight lines.

Shape and Form:

A large shape is heavier than a small one.

Squares tend to have more visual weight than circles; complex shapes have more visual weight than simple ones.

Organic shapes are visually heavier than geometric shapes.

Horizontal shapes are heavier than vertical ones.

Positive shapes have more visual weight than negative space.

Large forms are heavier than small ones.

Boost the visual weight of small objects by increasing their number. Two or more smaller forms will clump together to balance one large form.

Color:

Warm colors have more visual weight than cool colors.

Intense or bright colors are heavier than dull colors.

Dark colors are heavier than light ones—a smaller, darker shape can balance a larger, lighter one.

Black is the heaviest color, and white is the least visual weight.

Opaque areas have more visual weight than do transparent ones.

Texture and Pattern:

A textured or patterned form is heavier than a smooth form. You can tweak the balance by either adding or reducing the amount of texture and pattern in a given area.

Texture and pattern get their visual weight from changes in contrast.

Position:

Elements placed near the edge or corner of the composition appear heavier.

Objects located near the visual center of the design will balance those at the edge.

Like a parent and child on a seesaw, in order to balance, the parent must move toward the fulcrum while the child stays near the end.

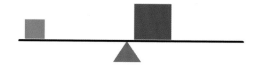

Whether the solution is simple or complex, successful balance is important for good design. It communicates much about an artwork and contributes to the overall tone, making a composition dynamic and lively, or restful and calm.

I love these asymmetrical earrings designed by Janis Kerman, because they have an immediate association as male and female figures. This communicates the idea that they are a balanced pair. Earrings are a good way to experiment with asymmetry. We really don't see both ears at the same time, at least not completely. So creating variations between earrings can be quite interesting. People will look back and forth to understand what they are seeing. This creates interest and is often a perfect conversation starter!

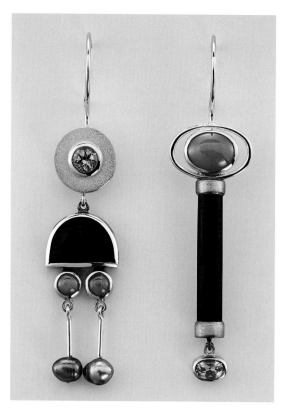

Janis Kerman. Earrings. Oxidized sterling, 18 kt. gold, onyx, coral, beryl, cultured pearl. 2009. Photo: Dale Gould.

Karen Gilbert uses color, texture, shape, contrast, and variety in this brooch. She creates balance by choosing lighter elements for the top and darker, denser beads at the bottom. The two metal flowers blend into one larger shape, which is simpler than the surrounding clusters, and therefore visually lighter. The other elements are the supporting cast in this piece. If you're not sure about the balance here, turn the book over and you'll see.

Karen Gilbert. "Catch" brooch. Sterling silver, glass seed beads, blown pyrex glass, topaz quartz, found ocean object, and copper. 2013. Artist photo.

BALANCE REQUIREMENTS
BY JEWELRY TYPE

Earrings: Mostly balanced around a vertical or radial axis. Try designing an asymmetrical pair.

Necklace: Center of balance is roughly halfway between jawline and the bustline.

Bracelet: Designed in the round. The biggest concern is physical balance. You don't want the focal area to drop to the bottom of the wrist.

Ring: More design freedom when it comes to balance. Try all types— symmetry, asymmetry, and radial. What about a multi-finger ring?

Brooch: The most freedom. Like small-scale sculpture. Just be sure it is physically balanced.

Balance Exercise:

Experiment with different types of balance. It's always advisable to experiment outside your comfort zone. It may not be successful at first, but it helps develop your critical abilities and adds to your range of expression.

If you have difficulty determining if your asymmetrical design is balanced, try these techniques.

Isolation: Use your hands or a viewfinder made from two L-shaped pieces of cardstock, to look at the design. This isolates the piece from the surrounding area. It focuses the attention and identifies any problems with the balance.

Reduction: Copy, scan, or take a black-and-white photo of the piece. This reduces the variables and makes it easier to evaluate visual weights, thus illuminating balance problems.

Reverse it: Change your point of view by turning the piece upside down. Or look at it in a mirror. This objectifies the composition, and any problems will immediately stand out.

Put it away: If none of these ideas has worked and you still are unsure about the balance, put it away for a while, a couple of weeks, or until your mental image of it has disappeared. When you take it out, your first impression will be correct. Trust it!

CONTRAST

Nature is full of opposites: light and shadow, rough and smooth, solid and lacy, for example. They exist in natural harmony with each other. There's nothing out of balance about a jumble of boulders beside a mountain stream. Twenty-four hours is the balance of day and night, and there's balance between a rough tree trunk and its delicate leaf canopy. A walk in the park will show you how pervasive contrast is. But why do we use it in art?

Contrast occurs when two dissimilar elements are put together. Emphasizing differences in color, value, size, and texture intensifies their impact. It draws and holds the viewer's attention. Artists also use contrast to direct attention to a particular part of a design, or to create a heightened sense of energy and emotion.

When you put contrasting elements together, it creates visual tension. The greater the difference, the greater the effect. As the saying goes, "Opposites attract!" The key to working with contrast is to make sure the differences are obvious. If it's too subtle, the effect is lost.

One high-contrast pair of opposites is black and white. The extreme difference makes this pairing very potent. This type of high contrast appears to come forward and seems to vibrate. High contrast is a significant tool for creating a dramatic atmosphere. Imagine a stormy night with flashes of lightning. A jagged line cuts through the darkness, and the effect is energy, emotion, and drama. High contrast also suggests duality in a more philosophical way: love and hate, peace and turmoil, good and evil, for example.

The paper necklace by Francesca Vitali shows how potent contrast can be. The juxtaposition of bright white and blood red makes for high drama. The artist interweaves the lines of color in a yin-yang fashion. The simplicity adds to the dramatic effect—one swoop of line in white and one in red. And there's the touch of print on the white paper, which makes us want to look closer. Dynamic, eye-catching, and powerful, this necklace is for the woman who wants to be noticed.

Francesca Vitali. "Connessioni" necklace. Repurposed paper, book pages, magnet clasp. 2012. Artist photo.

Make the most of all your design choices and decisions. Have a clear vision of the effect you want to achieve. Intention is the key. If you know where you want to go, you will find many ways to get there.

It is the common goal of every language, including visual expression, to convey meaning and express ideas, feelings, or beliefs. Contrast helps by organizing the information and improving the clarity of the message. It brings the viewer into the design, where the differences accentuate what the artist is trying to say. Choose the type of contrast that aligns with the mood you want to create. High contrast makes a piece vibrant and dramatic, while low contrast is quieter, more subtle, and soothing.

Amanda Denison has chosen a rugged textural contrast in this enameled necklace. The oxidized copper and white enamel are high contrast but easy on the eye and have both physical and visual texture. The patterns create movement as the eye jumps around the piece, while integrating the individual beads into a unified, rhythmic whole. The effect is organic, even earthy, as if the beads were excavated and restrung with contemporary materials. This gives the piece a bright, nuanced attitude that crosses a timeline.

Amanda Denison. "Tube Necklace." Liquid enamel on copper, oxidized sterling silver on black cotton rope. 2018. Artist photo.

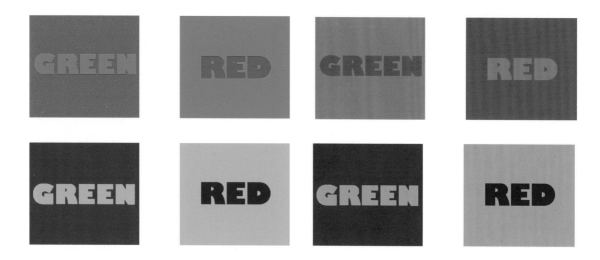

Color contrast creates visual pop and interest. When using complementary colors, you must consider value, which is the quality of darkness or lightness in the color. Without changing value, the contrast of complementary colors is counterproductive. Notice in the top left blocks above how the bold red and green create so much vibration that it is uncomfortable to look at. These two colors have the same value and intensity, as illustrated in the blocks to the right, where the hue is removed. Get more from the color

contrast by changing values. With the values changed, the vibration is lessened and the dynamism of contrast is much more effective.

Texture contrasts are especially effective in jewelry design. Shiny parts paired with matte or patinaed areas will make things pop, increase interest, and hold our attention longer than if all components have the same finish. Rough surfaces that abut smooth ones feel natural and engage our curiosity.

Choose contrast in shape and form. Pair round and square shapes or geometric ones

with organic forms. The differences increase the possibilities and make a design more compelling. There are so many ways to apply contrast in jewelry design; why not experiment and see what happens? As you look at the jewelry in this section, ask yourself how it makes you feel. Can you articulate what each piece is about? Is the message coming through? Why did the artist choose to use contrast? Would you react the same way without the contrast? Does this inspire you to incorporate contrast in your own work?

Céline Charuau created this necklace in polymer and metal. The entire design is about contrast. The contrasts are organic and geometric, red and green, two- and three-dimensionality, passive and active sides, and touchable and spiky. This is a very modern piece of jewelry that has a unique point of view and sends a clear message. Comparison and contrast are very effective.

Céline Charuau. "Ocotillo" pendant. Polymer, sterling silver. 2017. Artist photo.

Tamara Grüner works magic with disparate materials. This brooch has opposites galore! Rough and smooth, natural materials and man-made, solid and open, bright and dull color. As with the previous piece, when it comes to contrast, more is more. Although there is a lot going on, the artist has maintained balance and unity with consummate skill.

A variety of contrast is employed in this neckpiece by Teresa Faris. Color, texture, dimensionality, and closed versus open areas interact in unusual and compelling ways. The mustard-and-gray palette lowers the contrast, bringing harmony to the work. Notice the difference between the pieces with a variety of contrasts and those with just one. Some artists like many layers of design detail. Some of us prefer a solo vocalist, while others desire the harmony of many voices. Which do you prefer?

Tamara Grüner. "Savanna" brooch. Galalith, kyanite, oxidized silver, glass, plastic, paint, steel. 2016. Photo: Alexander König.

Contrast Exercise

1. How do you incorporate contrast in your work? Mix solid areas with open cutout parts, or solid forms with line? If you work in color, choose complementary colors or mix brights with neutrals. Everyone can contrast dark and light, large and small, or smooth and rough texture. It's time to get into the studio and do some experimenting. Remember to ask yourself, "What would happen if . . .?" Try something new. Change things around. Bring more drama—or maybe less.

2. Spend time looking at jewelry you love. Identify how, where, and what contrasts are in use and how it affects the design. Is contrast one of the things you love about the work? What is the emotional impact of the contrast? Does the contrast hold your attention and keep you engaged?

Teresa Faris. "Collaboration with a Bird II #13" necklace. Sterling silver, wood altered by a bird. 2012. Artist photo.

VARIETY

Variety, as the saying goes, is the spice of life. It's why we go on vacation. It's the deviation from our day-to-day lives that adds a spark of excitement. It sharpens our senses, makes us feel younger, and helps us experience things in a fresh new way. In art, variety adds that same renewed vitality and visual excitement.

Variety refers to a method of combining different elements to achieve intricate and complex relationships. It is used by artists who wish to increase the movement, rhythm, emotion, and energy in their work. Jewelry designs that include different hues, values, textures, shapes, and forms exhibit variety.

Varying the components in a design creates vivacity and cures monotony, but take care to convey a sense of cohesiveness. It is crucial to maintain harmony and clarity in the design. Without them, the composition will be a mess of mismatched ideas arranged in a haphazard way. How do we create unity out of diversity? To achieve a balance of unity and variety, the elements need to be alike enough that we perceive them as belonging together and different enough to be interesting.

This fabulous felt collar is by Danielle Gori-Montanelli. At first glance, there is a sense of playfulness and exuberance. Look at all the color, forms, shapes, and textures. There's a lot to take in. Although it makes an immediate impact, this is not a piece you can digest in a glance. Why does it work? We understand that these components represent succulents, which live in the same environment. In our minds, they are connected and belong together and therefore are unified and harmonious. There's no friction or discord putting them together in one composition.

Danielle Gori-Montanelli. "Succulents Collar" neckpiece. Felt. 2016. Photo: Lorenzo Gori-Montanelli.

The brooch by Ramón Puig Cuyàs shows how to get variety with shapes. The repetition of ovals in positive and negative space creates unity in the design. Color moves the eye around and through the composition and holds our attention. There is a strong interaction between two- and three-dimensionality in this piece. The combined effect is playful and modern, even though there is serious design work going on here. The artist keeps us involved as we keep looking for connections.

For example, take one particular shape and change the size, color, texture, and surface treatment. Let's choose a five-petaled flower as our example. Now make it in three different colors, five sizes, and use a variety of surface treatments. Unity is maintained through the repetition of one shape, and variety is created by the diversity of other elements.

You can accomplish the same effect with color. Choose a variety of shapes and sizes but keep them all in the one hue. This satisfies both principles—variety and harmony. Or use a theme to inspire object selection. The viewer will recognize the parts as a whole by their association, and the sense of connection will create harmony.

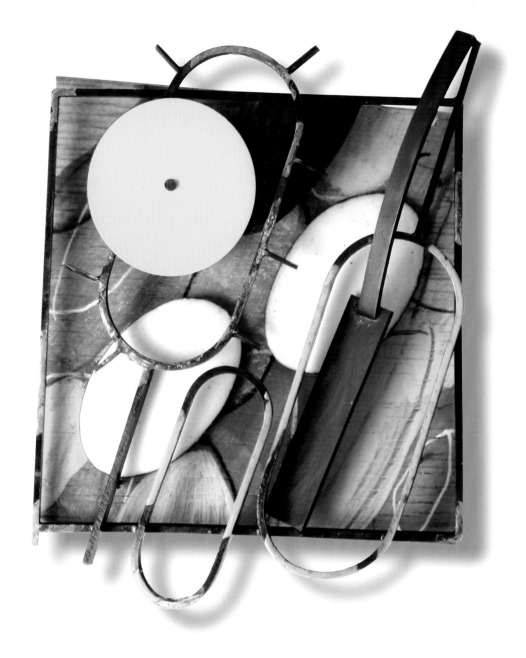

Ramón Puig Cuyàs. "El cactus creix lentamente N° 1458" brooch. Oxidized nickel silver, wood, enamel, plastic, paint. 2012. Artist photo.

Lorena Angulo works with the cultural iconography of her Mexican heritage. This necklace shows the rich variety of symbols: butterflies, crosses, flowers, hearts, and a skull. There is variety in texture and the materials too. It is organized as a traditional focal pendant that uses repetition and rhythm to create an organized, lucid composition. All the diverse components work harmoniously to support the theme. The narrative tells the universal story of life, death, and love.

Lorena Angulo. "Honoring" pendant. Bronze, onyx, red coral, pearls, dry flowers, rice, and resin. 2014. Photo: Victor Wolansky.

Variety is an uninhibited design principle. Keep a playful, festive attitude, when you use it. Designing with variety is effervescent—not serious. Variety works through juxtaposition and repetition. Where you position the repeated elements will create rhythm and movement in the design. It can be as simple as one repeated spot of red, or something with high contrast, which gets our attention and keeps us engaged.

Gail Crosman Moore is a master of variety. She works simultaneously in a number of media—metal, glass, felt, and resin—and isn't shy about mixing them together. There is always excitement and joy in her designs, as if her greatest pleasure is in breaking the rules! This bracelet combines handmade and vintage parts in a fanciful floral theme. The overall effect is fun and youthful. The artist chooses shapes to influence our gaze around and through the composition. The colors evoke warm, lazy summer days and parties after dark, when everything is in bloom.

Gail Crosman Moore. "Push and Pull Series" bracelet. Glass, vinyl, Lucite, steel. 2017. Artist photo.

Kathleen Dustin uses repetition of shape, color, and texture to create variety and unity in this necklace. Using essentially two shapes (a domed circle and an ovoid form), two colors (red and green), plus rough and smooth textures, there is a lot of variety in this design. Order is maintained by the strategic placement of the repeated elements and by the limitation of choices about what to repeat. This allows the playfulness to shine through. We are engaged in making connections, looking for all the greens, the circular parts, and the metal components. Variety keeps the audience excited and busy searching for connections.

Variety Exercise:

Now it's time to go into your studio. You probably have a stash of parts and pieces that didn't make it into a finished design. See what you can make using these disparate parts. Look for commonalities to create harmony. Are there "like" elements or beads of similar color? Is there a surface treatment or texture that could create unity out of diversity? Harmony is found in the things you choose to repeat. Look for similar elements that you can bounce around the design. Have fun. Enjoy the game. You might awaken a new feature for your art.

Kathleen Dustin. "Grass & Pods" necklace. Polymer, oxidized sterling. 2010. Photo: Charley Frieberg.

RHYTHM

Rhythm is timed movement through space, a clear path along which the eye follows a regular arrangement of motifs. It is a continuance, an undulation, or a tempo achieved by the repetition of regulated visual information.

When we think of rhythm we think of music or dance. We know the difference between marching and dancing. Marching is one step repeated at specific intervals. It's organized, orderly, and predictable. But it's only one beat. Rhythm is created when elements are repeated with variation. When you're moving your hips, torso, and arms along with your feet, you're dancing. The same principle applies to jewelry design. Picture a bracelet made of alternating black and white beads. The pattern goes around your wrist with a 1, 1, 1 beat, but it doesn't have rhythm. Change the bracelet by varying the order, shape, size, and texture of the beads. Now you have rhythm. Musical rhythm involves a beat that is repeated and varied over time. Visual rhythm is variation and repetition of design elements that move our view through the design space.

By repeating design elements in engaging ways, we create the interest and motion that are the first steps to establishing rhythm. Color makes a visual path from one component to another. Lines produce rhythm and imply motion. Forms create rhythm through their juxtaposition with each other. Rhythm requires repetition and patterning to achieve timed movement and a visual beat. Find the tempo that suits your inspiration, and the design elements that express that rhythm, and your intention will be clear.

A *regular rhythm* is created by repeating a series of identical or similar elements at

regular or comparable intervals. It is like the basic box step in dance, 4:4 time in music, and stripes or checks in a pattern. It is so predictable it can be monotonous, so spice it up with variety. Use different shapes or textures and play with less predictable repetitions. Have some fun, experiment, and see what kind of regular rhythms you can come up with.

Luis Acosta creates dramatic collars in stitched paper, using regular and alternating rhythms. Notice that the folded purple strip focuses the attention on the wearer's décolletage, while the polka-dot cones complete the piece with flourish. This simple, regular rhythm makes for a predictable, organized composition, but the artist's choices produce an exciting and unexpected visual experience.

Luis Acosta. "Ruff" necklace. Assorted paper, thread. Collection of Marianne Gassier. 2011. Artist photo.

The beaded bracelet by Julie Powell is a shining example of alternating rhythm. Notice the interplay between the patterned background and the smorgasbord of colored shapes on top. The eye travels back and forth on a visual path between colors, shapes, and textures. It is a lively, musical experience that is joyous and exuberant. How would you get this effect in your medium?

Julie Powell. "Boogie-Woogie Cuff" bracelet. Glass seed beads, embellished with olive jade, carnelian, lapis, turquoise, amazonite, pyrite, coral, and fire-polished glass. 2015. Photo: Larry Sanders.

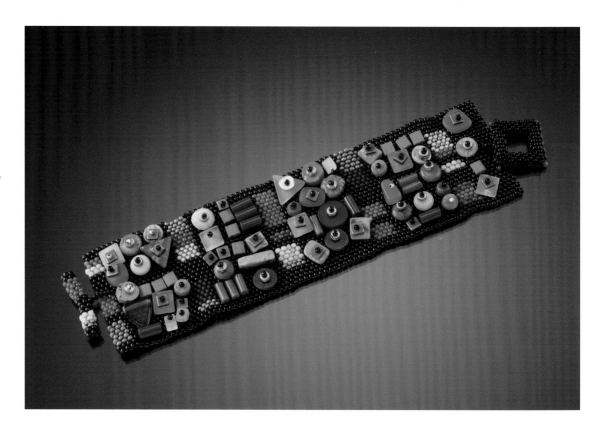

Alternating rhythm is created by combining two different regular rhythms or motifs. Imagine a chess board in black and red, with creamy-white pawns dotting the board in an obvious pattern. Your eye bounces between foreground and background patterns. Alternating rhythms create greater visual depth as we try to understand what's in front or on top. It's as simple as wavy, horizontal lines placed over straight, vertical ones, or as complex as you can imagine. In any case, alternating rhythms are compelling and anything but monotonous.

Scattering elements with no specific interval creates *random rhythm*, which is also called organic rhythm. This is what we see in nature. Cows dotted across a meadow, pebbles on a beach, clouds in the sky, or a starry night. We see and feel an underlying organization in nature that would be difficult to categorize. Random rhythm depicts an ebb and flow of elements or motifs, which feels natural and true. What seems random up close reveals a larger, purposeful order when viewed from a distance. Mimic this natural order with shapes, colors, or textures, and you achieve an intriguing, random rhythm. By envisioning the bigger picture, the possibilities are limitless.

Christel van der Laan is curious about rhythm. In this ring she uses three types of rhythm. The folded flaps in front have the random look of birds in flight. Behind that we see a regular pattern of holes. Plus the textured edge is another regular rhythm. By limiting her other choices to one material, color, and texture, we can focus on the rhythm story. This is smart design, simple and to the point. It makes a cohesive statement effectively and intentionally.

Christel van der Laan. "Reflex" ring. 18 kt. gold. 2010. Photo: Mei See Liang Jackson.

Progressive rhythm is a sequence of elements put together in a progression of steps. Each time the motif is repeated, it changes a little bit, morphing from one thing into another. This can be accomplished in many ways. Increasing the size of a repeated motif establishes progressive rhythm. The Doppler effect and the yellow brick road are examples. Create progressive rhythm by making incremental changes at consistent intervals. The component becomes bigger, bolder, and more vital to the design. Progressive rhythm can become the defining principle in a composition. It is a potent and dominant principle. Other principles and elements must remain secondary or the design becomes confusing. In this case, you have one star in the show, and everything else is the supporting cast.

One of my favorite things about creativity is how differently our minds and creativity work. I would never have imagined that zippers could produce the elegant rhythm and flow they do in this necklace. But Kate Cusack did. Your eye follows the toothed line of each zipper as it swirls and coils around itself. I'm reminded of a stream finding its way around boulders and settling into little whirlpools, or the sexy hairstyle of a classic movie star. The fact that the material is a zipper gives the piece a contemporary edge. It is feminine but not sweet. The unexpected material takes this piece to the next level.

Kate Cusack. "Tyres" necklace. Zippers, thread. 2007.
Photo: Frank Cusack.

Flow is created with undulating, curving motifs that twist and wave in natural ways. Flow is a sinuous, snaking, meandering path. It is the direct interpretation of natural rhythms we see in winding streams and falling leaves, the trails of waves on the sand, and windblown grasses. It expresses a gentle state of being. Flow is feminine, quiet, and dreamy. Use flow to convey these moods and feelings. There isn't a lot of drama or contrast in flow. Your palette should be cohesive, with colors that complement each other. Shapes should be organic and nestle together in a natural way. Textures should be easy and not coarse or harsh. Think of it as turning down the volume. Use gently curving and sensual lines to enhance the feeling of flow. Choose elements that are organic, comfortable, and nuanced. Unlike the progressive rhythm, flow works well with other principles. Pair it with balance, movement, or variety, and, of course, unity. Just remember is to keep the elements gentle and relaxed and you will create the kind of design that makes people sigh.

Rhythm produces order and predictability in a composition. Find your favorite rhythm and make the appropriate choices that will effectively communicate with your audience. Do you love hip-hop? Choose regular or alternating rhythms with bold shapes and high contrast for lots of energy and drama. Contemporary dance fans might choose alternating rhythms with plenty of highs and lows. Nature lovers go for random rhythm and flow, using soft curves and organic forms. Spend time analyzing the jewelry you love, to identify the rhythms that move you. It may inspire you to get up and dance.

Rhythm Exercise:

What is the rhythm of your soul? Take a look at your jewelry archives. How large a role does rhythm play in your work? Choose one or two pieces and redesign them to include rhythm. One easy way to do this is with tracing paper. Take a photo or make a black-and-white copy of the piece. Then, use the tracing paper to go over the shapes, moving elements around or changing the surface design to include rhythm.

The sensuous gentle curves in this bracelet by Nancy Linkin illustrate the mood and feeling produced by rhythm. The shapes evoke long, flowing curls; satin ribbons; or a soft, silky scarf. The eye follows the line, over and around the surface in a slow, smooth motion. The feeling in this piece is quiet, gentle, and contemplative. You can almost see a dancer sinuously moving her body through space. Creating this kind of emotional experience doesn't just happen. But if you set the intention and your creative choices support that idea, you will reach your goal.

Nancy Linkin. "Single Overlay Cuff." Patinaed and anticlastic formed bronze. 1995. Photo: Richard LaPalombara.

EMPHASIS

Emphasis creates a visual hierarchy and brings unity to the composition by pointing out what's important. Without unity or design dominance, you have a bunch of visual details but no story. If the design elements don't relate, and there's nothing pulling them together, they will be discordant and haphazard. Like a bunch of kids playing alone who become an organized whole when someone suggests a game they can play together. The organizing principle is necessary to make sense of the chaos.

Emphasis attracts the viewer's attention to a specific area or object. It makes a strong declarative statement and lets the viewer know where to pay attention and what is vital to the piece. It organizes the design around a dominant element, called the focal point, which could be color, texture, or shape, or a stone, enameled piece, or found object. It is common practice to place the focal point in areas that attract the most attention. That may be the visual center of the composition, but artists often choose a spot that is off to one side.

A focal point is a deviation from the surrounding area. It can be different in many ways. For example, a gorgeous stone offset by a decorative bezel, a piece of driftwood strung on geometric links, or a felted component mixed with glass beads. Pendants are an obvious example of a dominant focal point. Often, the focal element becomes the inspiration for the pendant. The focal piece is the North Star and the impetus for the creative process. All additional design decisions are made with it in mind; your hierarchy of importance is clear.

This ring by enamelist Julie Shaw shows how to use framing to create focus. The stone in the center is set apart and given more importance through the use of a decorative bezel. The saw-toothed bezel is repeated around the enamel and echoed in the texture of the backing piece as well. This repetition brings our eye from the edge to the center and back again. The artist distressed the enameled frame, linking it to the center color and pattern. This creates a centralized focal design that is modern and unusual.

Julie Shaw. Ring. Sterling silver, enamel, and acid-etched black onyx. 2015. Photo: Ryder Gledhill.

Here's a great example of anomaly. Can you imagine walking through the woods and looking down at the fallen leaves to see an ancient coin? Neither can I. It is the juxtaposition of these two things that establishes the focus in this brooch by Patrik Kusek. The coin is in the visual center of the composition. The branches, leaves, and tendrils swirl around it but do not point to it. The gold of the coin helps contribute to its importance, and yet it doesn't arrest our attention. There is enough interest in the color, shape, and movement of elements around the coin to create a unified, fascinating, and harmonious piece.

A piece of jewelry may have more than one area of emphasis. However, one typically dominates any others. If two focal areas have equal importance, the eye bounces back and forth, unsure of where to look and trying to solve the puzzle. Reestablish clarity by diminishing the importance of other design elements. If your main focal piece is brightly colored, large, and shiny, then your secondary focal area should be duller, smaller, and matte. When a hierarchy of focus is in place, all parts are there to support the primary element. This reduces confusion and leads to better enjoyment of the piece.

Contrast is a good way to create emphasis. The greater the contrast between the focal element and the surrounding components, the greater attraction for our attention. Imagine a necklace of stunning cadet-blue beads, with one vermillion bead among them. It's easy to envision how easily that red bead draws our gaze, even if the contrasting bead is smaller and set off to one side. Contrast can be produced with value, texture, pattern, size, and material.

Anomaly establishes visual pop because it is wildly different from the whole. A perfect square amid a group of organic forms will certainly demand our attention. An anomaly doesn't blend in; instead, it breaks the rules. It is the juxtaposition of things not normally seen together. Contrast and anomaly together are good ways to add freshness and surprise to your designs.

Patrik Kusek. "The Memory Interrupted Series" brooch. Sterling and fine silver, 22 kt. gold. 2016. Photo: Abby Johnston.

Another way to produce focus and emphasis is *isolation*. Take one item out of a group and move it to another part of the composition. This causes us to look from the group to the individual and back again. It makes the isolated element have more impact, and creates visual tension in the design. When using this technique, do not add any elements that interfere with the isolated piece. Let the isolated element draw the attention, and let the viewer reflect on the relationships.

Convergence is the technique of creating pointers to direct our attention to the focal point. This approach is very powerful. Using shapes, lines, or colors from many directions to point toward the focal area creates a strong gravitational pull. It is difficult to look away from the focal area. Convergence sets up radial symmetry, like a flower or snowflake, which is an almost unbreakable bond. Because the pull of convergence is so potent, use it sparingly and intentionally.

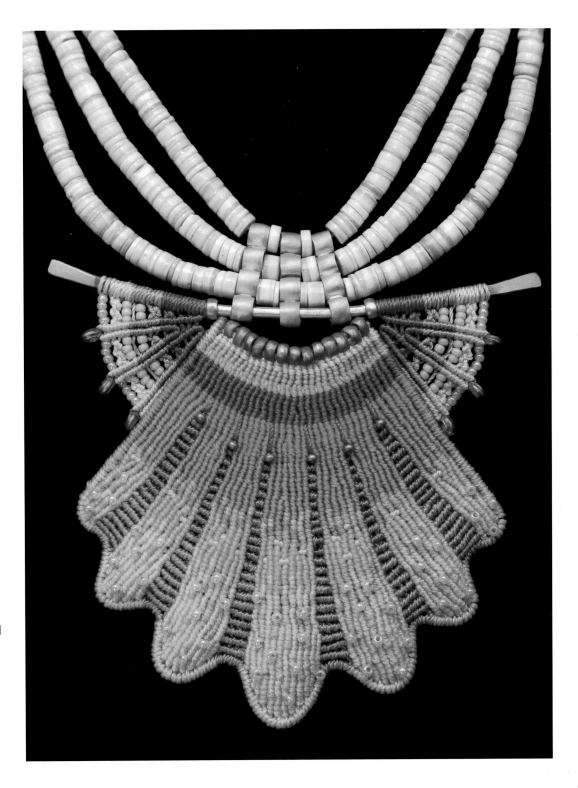

The focal pendant by Joan Babcock creates focus with convergence. The piece has a symbolic universality that allows each viewer to engage their own perspective. Is it a version of a Native American motif, a reflected sunrise, or a floral design? The focal piece flows outward in rays of line and color as our view returns to the crescent-shaped negative space. The stacked copper beads draw our eyes up to the necklace strands and back again to repeat the visual path. This is a reminder that focal emphasis can be a positive or negative space.

Joan Babcock. "Seashell Series #1" pendant. Nylon cord, glass beads, copper, melon shell heishi. 2007. Photo: Jeffrey Babcock.

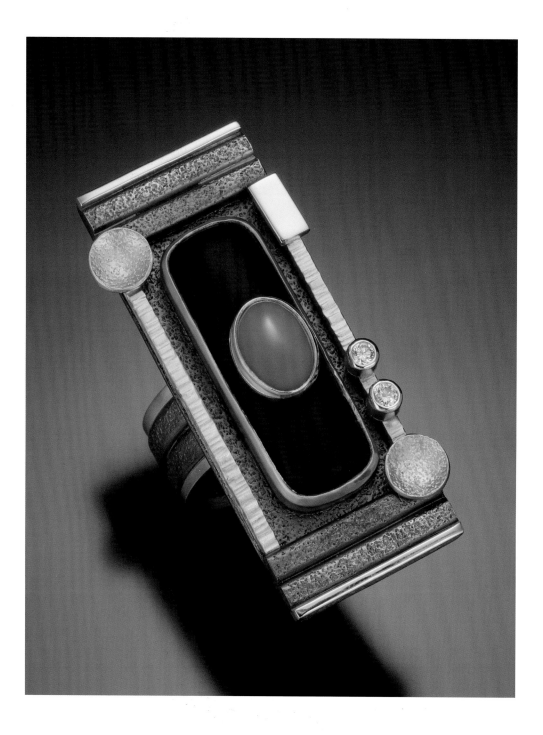

Where is the emphasis in this ring by Beth Solomon? The primary focus is the central cabochon. But it is not alone. The black jade creates a larger focal area by merging with the coral. The attention now moves to the four circular elements. The gold discs and diamonds are divided as a grouping of three with one disc in isolation. This creates good movement and builds a much-stronger design story. In this way, a hierarchy develops in which each element has its place and the artist's intention is clear.

You can highlight your focal area by framing it. *Framing* includes everything from bezels to borders; anything that surrounds the focal point and enhances it. Framing your dominant element elevates its importance. We frame things that are special, precious, and beautiful. Consider all the ways you could show off your focal point with framing. After all, creativity is really creative problem-solving.

So where do you put your most important or dominant item? Position is critical to support the focus you are setting up. In necklaces, rings, and brooches, the strongest position is in the visual center of the composition. It's a natural spot for the eye to begin exploring the design, as well as a place for the eye to rest and reflect. It establishes design dominance, stability, and unity. This is one reason why so much jewelry is symmetrically balanced around a central focus. In necklace design, it also directs focus to a woman's most alluring jewelry zone, from the base of the neck to the décolletage. It's an obvious area to draw attention to.

Beth Solomon. "Rectangular Coral and Matte Black Jade Ring." Sterling, 18 kt. and 22 kt. gold, white diamonds, matte black jade, natural red coral. 2009. Photo: Robert Diamante.

Emphasis is a powerful design tool. It teaches us how to affect the viewer and direct their attention. It demands that we create a hierarchy of importance within a composition. It produces unity and harmony among the elements and makes communication and comprehension easier. Emphasis is at times very subtle, and at other times—bold. Remember, if too many things are highlighted, nothing will stand out. The effect you're trying to create will be negated, and your meaning will be obscured. When you make conscious choices about what is important, and direct the viewer's attention there, your design story is strong and clear. As you go through this book, notice how each piece of art directs your gaze. How did the artist achieve this? What did they want you to see first? How do you respond to the various types of emphasis?

Focal points do not have to be centered or flashy. Look at these brooches by Ruth Ball. These quiet, unified designs have a tender quality that would be ruined by a bold, high-contrast focal point. The artist instead chooses gold cloisonné wire to create the focal points. On the right-hand piece, it is the circle in the lower third of the design. But where is it in the left-hand piece? Is it the large arc on the left side or the little circle in the upper right? Which do you see first? Where does your gaze return to? There's no right or wrong answer. But analyzing how you react to the artistic choice teaches you a lot about jewelry design.

Ruth Ball. "Long Pebble Brooches." Vitreous enamel on silver, gold cloisonné wire. 2012. Artist photo.

Focal Point Exercise:

Creating effective focal points is a skill every artist should have at their disposal. Let's reinforce the information with a couple of exercises.

1. Build your focal point: Using drawing materials, paper shapes, Colorforms®, or a drawing app, create a variety of shapes to play with. Choose contrast, anomaly, isolation, convergence, or framing to create a pleasing design with an obvious focal point. Take a photo, use tracing paper, or copy it on your printer. You want to have copies to compare later to other options. Try this with several of the methods and consider which you like best.

2. Identify your focal point: Using decorative paper, magazines, and newspapers, cut up about ten shapes. Arrange them on a blank sheet until you are pleased with the collage. Glue the shapes in place. Make a viewfinder. Cut two pieces of plain paper into large "L" shapes. Flip one over to create a rectangular opening. Move the viewfinder over the collage, looking for interesting arrangements with focal interest. Record your solutions for later analysis.

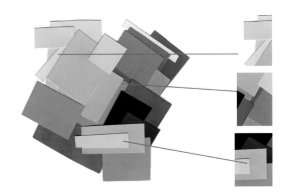

PROPORTION

Proportion is usually taken for granted. Often we don't even notice it unless something is out of harmony. When the comparable size of the elements seems wrong, odd, or uncomfortable, we say the composition is out of balance or disproportionate. Proportion is the relative size of the parts of a design. It is discussed in terms of a context or standard used to determine pleasing proportions. What is that standard? And how do you know what size the parts should be? The standard for what constitutes good proportions is one of beauty, harmony, and balance. Proportion is how we know when something is beautiful.

Once you understand the inherent balance in good proportion, you will surely recognize them in this brooch from Keith Lewis. Examine the relationships, the way the space is broken up and allocated to the different materials, and the ratio of black to gold, and gold to the accent components. Everything has been considered and skillfully arranged. Our initial impression is simplicity, but upon reflection we see the strategic decisions the artist made to achieve this end.

Keith Lewis. "Oval Anthracite Brooch." Anthracite, opal with matrix, ruby, pearls, goldleaf, and mica. 2012. Photo: Ralph Gabriner.

Good proportion is like a wonderful meal, in which no one ingredient overwhelms our taste buds. There are different amounts of sweet and tart, chewy and crunchy. When the elements come together in the right amounts, the food is delicious, but when there's too much salt . . . the dish is ruined. A recipe lists exactly how much of each ingredient is needed to make a yummy dish, but where is the recipe in art?

Historically, most cultures have an agreed-on standard of beauty. There are standards for art, architecture, landscape design, fashion, and, of course, for human beauty, in face and form. Euclid is credited with being the first person to study perfect proportional relationships in geometric shapes. Over time this concept has come to be known as the golden ratio. During the Renaissance, the idea experienced a resurgence, and artists, notably Leonardo da Vinci, began to apply the idea to painting and sculpture. Since that time, the golden ratio has helped artists define aesthetically pleasing proportions. It is used to analyze everything from seashells to the human face. The more closely the proportions follow this ratio, the more beautiful the object is considered to be. The Fibonacci spiral is a visual representation of the mathematical principle. As an arc dissects each section, a spiral is created. It neatly illustrates the complex mathematical equation $1 + 1/\varphi = \varphi$.

For our purposes, we can discuss the principle without engaging the precise math involved.

In the diagram you will notice that the whole is divided roughly into ⅔ and ⅓ sections. The smaller section is subdivided into ⅔ and ⅓ over and over again. The Fibonacci spiral shows that harmony is achieved by repeating this division. This rule will successfully guide you in choosing the most pleasing sizes for the elements in your designs.

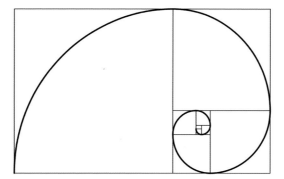

This cuff bracelet by Sydney Lynch shows how harmony is created with the golden ratio. The band is divided into three segments. The bottom segment is approximately ⅓ of the top part, while the middle segment is about ⅓ of the bottom part. The gold certainly takes up ⅓ of the cuff, while the large stone is ⅓ of the gold.

Sydney Lynch. "Cuff" bracelet. Koroit boulder opal, spessartite garnet, 18 kt. and 22 kt. gold, oxidized silver. 2016. Photo: Alan Jackson.

The specific size relationships you should pay attention to are length, width, and breadth of the elements; the space between and around elements; and the size of one area of the design in relation to another. Choose which will be the larger, dominant portion (⅔ part) and which is the smaller, ⅓ part. Dividing the smaller bit the same way will give you the accent elements for your design. This will create design dominance and produce harmonious proportions.

You will also get good results by grouping similar elements together. Elements such as color, texture, and shape can be arranged with the ratio in mind to create dynamic compositions. Apply the concept to the distribution of positive and negative space in the design. However you apply it, the golden ratio will create a more harmonious and beautiful design.

Dividing a composition into equal parts such as halves or quarters can easily become monotonous. This division of space is traditionally avoided in painting or photography, but this kind of division is often used in jewelry. It creates a solid geometry on which to arrange your elements; it creates symmetry, balance, and simplicity. It produces a design space for arranging interesting surface treatments. Regular geometric shapes make up a considerable percentage of all jewelry designs. Keeping proportion in mind will add interest and sophistication to the simplest form.

In this pendant, goldsmith Steven Kolodny creates proportional relationships between the large drusy and the gold elements that surround it. The skillful proportions give this design a feeling of balance and unity. Notice the repeated proportion in the gold elements. There are roughly ⅔ and ⅓ segments in each of the gold elements. The repetition is subtle and does not jump out at you. But once you notice it, you see how it creates order and harmony. Your eye easily moves from one part of the design to another and is never met with disproportion.

Steven Kolodny. "Poseidon's Amulet" pendant. Drusy chryscolla, blue stick pearl, blue apatite, 18 kt. gold. 2013. Photo: Ralph Gabriner.

The rule of thirds is another common concept for creating good proportion in your work. This technique suggests that you divide the design space into nine equal portions by using two equally spaced horizontal lines and two equally spaced vertical lines. The rule proposes that important compositional elements should be placed along these lines or at their intersections. By aligning important design elements with these points, you create more tension, energy, and interest in the composition.

This brooch by Lorena Angulo illustrates how to use the rule of thirds in jewelry. Notice that the design elements are arranged within the imaginary nine-square grid. The spiral motif travels along the horizontal lines, the angel's wings attach at the junction of verticals and horizontals, and the butterfly has conformed nicely to the central square. The placement of these elements creates balance, order, harmony, and good proportion.

This beaded necklace by Sandy Swirnoff is an example of establishing proportion with elements other than size. By using just three colors she has created a graphic and dramatic story. Adding pattern has effectively created a fourth color. So the color hierarchy is black, white, black-and-white patterned areas, and orange. Without the black-and-white patterned parts, the amounts of black and white would be too similar and the orange would seem disproportionate. That little bit of pattern creates a bridge that brings all the proportional relationships into harmony.

Lorena Angulo. "Mariposa Reina" brooch. Bronze. 2013. Photo: Robert Diamante.

Sandy Swirnoff. "Fiber Hat Dance" necklace. Seed beads, hand-fired glass discs, Bakelite button, black onyx beads, fiber, rubber cord. 2010. Artist Photo.

SCALE

Scale refers to the size of an object in relation to another object. In jewelry that means the size of the jewelry in relation to the human body. We evaluate the size of jewelry pieces on the body and define them as small, medium, large, or even enormous. Which size is right? The scale of jewelry is something that is routinely reexamined.

It is often a question of fashion trends. At times, jewelry is small and dainty; at other times, large and dramatic.

Art jewelers today are pushing the envelope when it comes to size. It is the vanguard to see necklaces that engulf the torso, earrings that hang below the shoulder line, and bracelets that climb up the forearm. Many of these pieces are designed to stretch the definition of jewelry as a functional art form. The artist may also be making a political statement or trying to shock the viewer. This unconventional work makes you question your preconceived notions about the significance of jewelry in modern culture.

How big is too big? How heavy is too heavy? How much does wearability matter? What are the parameters for different types of jewelry? These are interesting and debate-worthy conversations. It is important to stay curious, question set ideas, and stay open to what's new and different. Spend some time examining cutting-edge jewelry. Take notice of trends and ideas outside your comfort zone. Identify the pieces that you reject instantly. What is it about a piece that turns you off? What feelings does it bring up?

What qualities do you find ugly or offensive? Analyzing art that you don't like is as informative as looking at pieces you love. Where does your work fall on the continuum from traditional to unconventional?

For jewelry designers, size matters when jewelry is too big to function. Is it too heavy, does it pull on fabric, or does it hang heavily on the neck or earlobes? Does it get in the wearer's way or interfere with clothing? Can you wear a coat over it? Is it dangerous, with sharp, pointy edges?

The question is how closely you want to follow trends. What is your personal size

aesthetic? I love big, bold pieces and often wonder what I will do when smaller jewelry is fashionable again. Once you identify your preferred scale and the current trends, you might want to experiment with your designs. Are you designing for your own body size? Women come in all shapes and sizes. The size of the jewelry they choose often corresponds more to their personalities and how much of an impact they want to make than it does to their physiques. Some very small women like large "statement" pieces, while bigger women often prefer daintier jewelry. It's not the size of the woman—it's the woman inside!

Genevieve Williamson. "Antarctic" earrings. Polymer, sterling, and acrylic paint. 2014. Artist photo.

How big is too big? How big do you think these earrings by Genevieve Williamson are?—1 ½ inches or 4½ inches? The brilliant thing about this design is its sense of monumentality. The bold, simple shapes and textures have a universal quality that would be just as effective if they fit in your palm or as sculpture in a city center. When we don't know the size of a piece of art, it allows us to stretch our minds and imagination to the possibilities of scale.

The trend for large-scale jewelry is apparent in these two examples of abundant necklace designs.

Maud Villaret's dramatic fiber and beaded collar combines bold colors and high contrast. Variety, pattern, texture, and color create an air of exuberance, which is contained by the strict organization of the elements. Cécile Bertrand layers large ribbon beads to create this dramatic look. Is it too much? Absolutely not. The limited palette and regular rhythm keep everything under control, but the scale is grand. However, please note the importance of lightweight materials. These pieces would be unwearable were they made in thick metal and heavy stones. The increasing number of jewelers working in alternative materials has had a real impact on current scale trends.

Left: Maud Villaret. "Redsun" collar. Wax Vlisco fabric, bazin, bronze beads, cowrie shells, brass chain, glass beads, leather, Swarovski crystals, turquoise beads, magnet clasp. 2014. Photo: Stéphane Pironon.

Above: Cécile Bertrand. Necklaces. Black satin, silver linen, thread. 2015. Artist photo.

It is a crucial part of the creative process to continually ask "What if?" and "Why not?" How can you use the cutting edge of design ideas to stretch and inform your vision? What new concepts can you incorporate into your repertoire? How would your work change if it were 25 or 50 percent bigger? Does the very suggestion make you feel anxious? Maybe you are playing it safe. It could be time to start experimenting with scale to see what happens.

Here is a side-by-side comparison of one of the most common of all jewelry designs, the gemstone ring. Goldsmith Isabelle Posillico has designed a unique, elegant, and modern ring. It is gorgeous, with high quality both in design and craftsmanship, and it looks very wearable. The artist uses texture, shape, form, and spatial relationships to establish unity, movement, and balance. Philip Sajet's ring has the same high quality in artistry, but it also has showstopping drama. The artist employs the same design elements to a very different result. The scale makes this ring unexpected and theatrical. This is a ring you want people to notice, and they will, mostly because of its size. Which of these beautiful designs are you more attracted to? Which one would you like to try on right now? Which one gives you design ideas and makes you want to get into your studio?

Isabelle Posillico. "Road Trip" ring. 18 kt. gold, .45 ct. diamonds. 2006. Photo: Hap Sakwa.

Philip Sajet. Ring. 18 kt. gold, rutilated quartz. CODA
Collection, Apeldoorn, The Netherlands. 2003. Artist photo.

Scale Exercise:

See how much size matters. Take an actual-sized picture
of a current piece. With your printer, increase the size by
20, 50, or even 100 percent. Cut out the photocopy
and put it on or against your body. What kind of
statement does it make? Does it have more presence and
potency? Or does it seem big and clunky? Now try
going the other way. Take the original and shrink it by
20 percent or more. Is it more personalized and
precious? Do the elements seem more valuable or exotic?
Or does it look inconsequential? If this experiment gives
you a creative nudge, maybe it's time to push the scale
of your work.

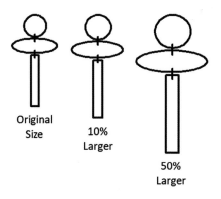

PART THREE

Putting It
Together

We've done the personal archeology to find our unique inspiration, learned about the importance of process and function, and discovered how to use the elements and principles of design. That's a lot of information. How do you put it all together to make better jewelry? Don't worry, there's a plan for that. Learning how to use these tools is necessary to know which one each job requires. If the design is about stress and agitation, you now know the lines and textures that express those feelings. Perhaps you're dreaming of the serenity you experience high up in the mountains. Choose the rhythms and patterns that set that particular tone.

To put it all together, you need a system. A design hierarchy is a system that assigns a level of importance to all the design parts. Deciding what's most important will guide your choices and bring each composition to fruition. It's all in your hands.

The purpose of this book is not to establish hard-and-fast rules, but to illustrate the possibilities. What you choose to focus on is part of "finding your voice." Your voice is the integration of design information in a unique and personal way, creating a signature look, one that is recognizable across a body of work. This book contains the guidance to help you find your voice.

At the end of our journey is critique. A singularly important skill, critique is how we learn from every piece we make. It is the assessment and analysis of our work that ensures that our intention and meaning are clear. When you can confidently give and receive solid critique, you have successfully integrated the concepts and vocabulary of art and design.

Andy Cooperman. "Medusa" pendant. Sterling, 18 kt. gold, diamonds. 2003. Photo: Doug Yaple.

DESIGN HIERARCHY

From the moment of inspiration, when the kernel of an idea pops into your head, you begin making choices. You decide what's most important about your current design. Is it balance or contrast, rhythm or scale? You must choose what's most important to clearly tell your story. If you are going to make a chocolate cake, you need chocolate. You wouldn't want friends saying, "Delicious cake, but what flavor is it?" The most important thing is that it's a *chocolate* cake.

A design hierarchy is the organization of design features into levels of relative importance. It establishes a framework for the parts of the composition. It communicates what the piece of jewelry is about. You can generally sum up this primary aspect in one or two words. Take a random look at some of your favorite jewelry pieces in this book. Choose a word or two to describe each piece. You'll notice that one artist is interested in texture, while another is curious about spatial relationships, and the third may be all about balance.

How do you know what each artist is interested in? They have selected a principle or element to be the dominant feature of that piece. Ideas and design components were sorted into strata to create a clear structure

What is the fundamental story in this necklace? Kathleen Dustin has created a rich, nuanced design that is all about pattern and texture. Dots and lines, incised or layered—patterns are picked up, moved around, and repeated on each bead. Pattern and texture dominate this piece. So much so that color, balance, and even movement are of lesser importance.

Kathleen Dustin. "Tribal Barrel Necklace." Polymer and magnetic clasp. 2016. Photo: Charley Frieberg.

and order. Working with all the resources in the design toolbox—the elements and principles—the content of the composition is organized and prioritized. Visual hierarchy influences the order in which we perceive what we see. The principle of dominance helps in establishing this order.

The dominant element usually has the most visual weight. It is the element of primary emphasis, and therefore it is what we notice first. This is usually a focal point or area. Although it may be what we notice first, it is not the most essential part of the composition. The dominant element grabs our attention, but the hierarchy gives the design its structure. These two concepts are at the core of good jewelry design. All other principles and elements work toward supporting them.

The dominant component serves as our way into the design. It advances to the foreground of the composition, usually due to contrast, placement, or repetition, but it could also be size, color, texture, etc. The more pronounced the visual weight, the more dominant the element. Dominance is fairly easy to understand. A quick look at most compositions easily identifies the dominant element.

What is the visual hierarchy of this brooch by Andrea Williams? Rhythm or movement, shape, and texture. The component parts—the dark petals, gold silk cocoons, and white sapphires—are arranged in a rhythmic way. It evokes leaves or seashells scattered on the ground. The petal shapes are the dominant feature, but rhythm or movement is what it's all about. It would have a very different feeling if the shapes were geometric. There is a universal appeal to the way Mother Nature arranges things. It is the artist's job to pay close attention and translate the experience for the viewer. The artist's choices here have arranged the parts in a clear and meaningful way.

Andrea Williams. Brooch. Reclaimed sterling silver, lab-grown white sapphires, and wild silk cocoons. 2016. Photo: Mark Craig.

Be aware of how each of your elements interacts with the adjacent parts and the design as a whole. Design flow is created by selecting principles and elements that support the main concept. Our brains can easily distinguish between the largest amount and the smallest, plus one or two levels in between. Without even realizing it, we rank the parts of a design from crucial to unnecessary, on the basis of their visual weight and contribution to the whole. But keep your hierarchy to three or four levels, or it will become visually confusing and difficult to comprehend.

If you are making Gramma's chicken soup, the main ingredient is the chicken. You want big chunks of meat in a delicious broth so your family can savor the sweet, fresh taste of poultry. The second layer is the vegetable mix. The mirepoix adds the fullness of texture and color and enhances the flavor of the broth. Finally, add the herbs and spices. Not too much, because they pack a punch, but your soup would be bland without them. The aroma may be what draws us in, but it is the well-balanced flavors of the soup that leave us satisfied.

Remember this when designing jewelry. And ask yourself these questions: What is my main focus? Will the viewer understand what this piece is about? Have I chosen the best elements and principles to communicate the idea? Do the choices I've made support the main concept and does anything detract from it?

The human form or image always takes primacy in a design, as in this piece by Bettina Speckner. We can't help but be drawn to it. It begins an internal dialogue, as we find ourselves asking questions about this person's story. With this in mind, how would you create a more captivating experience? This artist uses a balance of geometric shapes to move our view around the composition. The twin ovals, one positive and one negative, establish a strong dynamic tension. This is critical to the unity of the piece. The gentleman is staring out of the picture plane, and we would follow his gaze unless a powerful force pulls us back. The two ovals do just that. Finally, the neutral palette gives the design an aged, homogenous feel.

Bettina Speckner. Brooch. Ferrotype: photo etching in zinc, silver, pearls. 2011. Artist photo.

VISUAL HIERARCHY

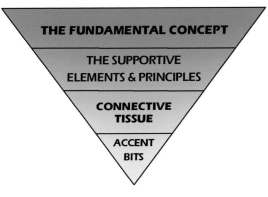

| THE FUNDAMENTAL CONCEPT |
| THE SUPPORTIVE ELEMENTS & PRINCIPLES |
| CONNECTIVE TISSUE |
| ACCENT BITS |

Establish a visual hierarchy and let the structure tell the design story. Choose three zones of importance: primary, secondary, and tertiary. As previously noted, the primary level of importance should be obvious and pervasive. The elements of secondary emphasis will become the middle ground of your design, while the tertiary level is given the least visual weight. Subordinate elements should recede into the background of the composition. They are the connective tissue that unifies the more important parts. Add a fourth level only if needed. In the soup analogy, this would be a garnish. It's just a pinch of something unusual, cilantro or nutmeg. One small note—a color or a shape—that is in high contrast to the overall tone. This adds pop and sizzle to the design.

Take a look through this book. These masterful works display a sense of order, and the consciousness of decision-making. The artists set out to express specific thoughts and feelings and have gauged their design decisions on that primary focus. If there were a lack of dominance in these designs, there would be confusion and competition between the parts. Our interaction with the design would be difficult and unsatisfying—not at all like Gramma's chicken soup.

These two pieces talk about balance and contrast. The necklace is by Katja Prins. Contrast is the dominant feature: between the red and white parts, and the flat versus three-dimensional elements. But the theme is balance. The artist uses placement, size and shape, and clustering and isolation to establish asymmetrical balance. So the hierarchy consists of balance, contrast, and color. Olga Ledneva uses shape, color, and texture to create balance. The strong vertical background balances the large green form, while the bright-yellow leaf vertically balances the piece so it doesn't feel top heavy. Can you see the similarities in the pieces? How does your gaze move around each one? Notice how the focal points keep us coming back to rest. Comparing and contrasting different pieces of jewelry is an excellent practice. It hones your analytical skills.

Olga Ledneva. "Flower Brooch." Polymer clay, metal accents, and a magnetic clasp. 2018. Artist photo.

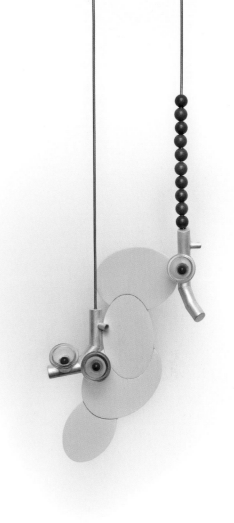

Katja Prins. "Inter-Act" pendant. Sterling, reconstructed red and white coral, glass, and steel. 2012. Photo: Harold Strak.

FINDING YOUR VOICE

What does it mean when artists talk about voice? And why is it important? Your voice is that quantifiable something about your work that is recognized by others. It is a mixture of message, style, and technique that is uniquely yours. Your voice is the amalgam of your character, interests, beliefs, emotions, and everything that makes you unique. Your life story is the tone of your body of work.

It's not something you can find at a workshop or in a book. You cannot find it outside yourself, because your voice is you. Students often tell me that they are not interesting or unique enough and they don't have anything deep to say. This is the full-circle moment in this book and in mastering jewelry design. Because to find your voice you have to be in touch with what inspires you, thrills you, and piques your curiosity. Through quiet reflection and active pursuit, get to know what thrills you. Read or listen to podcasts, be alone in nature or as part of the multitudes in a city, sing and dance, or play tennis—experience life!

Your voice is already within you. We call it "finding your voice" rather than choosing it or making it up. Many times, before we realize it ourselves, others will notice it in our work. Sometimes it sneaks up on us in the midst of making things. Suddenly you will feel called to take a slightly different path. That's your voice calling you in a more intimate direction.

Just as in any kind of self-discovery, you need to ask yourself questions. Be specific and honest about the answers. We all love nature, but what part of that vastness speaks to you? Plants or animals, large or small, land, sea, or air? You are doing some personal archeology, excavating your life for clues about yourself, and on a treasure hunt to find what turns you on and what you're curious about. Here are some common trail markers for the journey.

Melanie West. "Horned Bangle in Blue" bracelet. Hollow-formed polymer with hand-pigmented cane lamination. 2017. Artist photo.

INSPIRATION

Carry your journal or sketchbook with you. Make it a daily habit to record things that jump out at you. A quick note or sketch, a bunch of random words, a song or sound carried on the wind: capture the things that are meaningful to you. It may not make sense at first, but a pattern will emerge as you collect the data. Your interests will become clear and point you in the next direction.

This is a "getting to know you" phase, so it's a good idea to detach from other people's art. Go on an internet diet. We are overwhelmed with visual stimuli on the internet, and everyone making jewelry uses it as a platform. It can be intimidating and frustrating. If you see your ideas as a trend or in someone else's work, it will stifle your creativity. Better to unplug from technology and plug in to yourself and your unique inspiration.

Take a good look at your past work—all of your creative work both in and out of the studio. Banish the internal messages that tell you what you should be doing. This will free you from limitations and allow you to create more authentic art. Work to shake off feelings of unworthiness. You are about to take a leap of faith, and you must believe in the possibilities to succeed.

Katie Schutte. "Sabellida Motif" collar. Crocheted and powder-coated wire. 2010. Photo: Jeff Sabo.

When you have the kernel of an idea about the direction your voice is calling from, follow it. You may not have a clear vision yet, but there are clues. Fascination and curiosity are two big clues. Take the journey of discovery, build the skills you need, take a class, learn a technique, or try a new tool. Is your voice clearer now? Are you getting more ideas? Keep going. Look for ways to visually express your ideas and feelings. Question, experiment, and play. Fail and get back up again. Analyze your work and your progress on this path. Is it successful and is it worth doing?

LEARN FROM A PERSONAL MASTER

Now is the time to look for an art hero—someone whose work moves you and makes you want to be better. Someone you can learn from, either technically or artistically. Meet this person if you can, listen to their thoughts, read what they have written, and study their work. Part of our art education has always been to copy masterworks. It helps us understand how the design parts come together to create our experience of the work. We learn by emulating or mimicking the work while we hone our technical and expressive skills.

Remember that imitating is practice, not the end goal. It's an avenue for finding your personal direction. But you will have to put the copying down to do your own work. It is a risk, and risks do feel risky. You want to develop a unique, authentic voice, so you must do the work. It's time to move to the next level, taking these new insights, tools, and skills to your very own place.

BLOSSOMING

You have achieved a solid level of mastery over the skills you need to make good jewelry. You have done the self-inquiry and followed in the footsteps of the masters. You know what you want to say and how to say it. Now's the time to begin taking the risk of telling your own story and making your voice heard. People will notice and respond. You gain confidence. Your work gets better and more personal. You are on your own path, creating identifiable work that's well designed and finely crafted. And it feels fabulous. You take more risks and leaps of intuition and your voice broadens and deepens. This is a wonderful place to be, and you will get comfortable here. Too comfortable!

GETTING STUCK

Once you find that combination of message, style, and technique that is your voice, you relish being there and you begin to want to protect the thing you've become known for. You rework the ground, finding variations and nuances within your body of work. It's nice to be in your own little corner of the world. It's comforting and comfortable. But it's also easy to stagnate there, to stop hearing your creative voice and lose your thirst for new inspiration. All the chances you took and all the self-discovery have become second nature. And one day you wake up itching for change. What do you do now?

"How do I break out of this comfort zone? What if the next path doesn't work for me? What about my collectors? How will they respond to the new directions I want to explore? What if I fail? What new opportunities do I want to pursue with my work? How can I protect what I've done, while striving for something new?"

When we get stuck in the creative doldrums, retelling the same story over and over, we need to start the process again. Go inside; remember what you love, get curious, and start looking at the world anew. This is one of the times that your sketchbook or journal is vital. You can revisit ideas that you didn't explore before. Look for the road not taken and this time . . . take it.

Then try new techniques. Look at artists who have explored this new arena, and learn from them. Dive deep and do that personal excavation. Find out what you have to say about this new subject. Listen closely and pay attention to the voice you hear. It is your voice.

Artist Jan Smith:

In art school, one of my professors told us to do what you know. In my artistic practice, I investigate concepts that evolve from an intimate connection to place and reflect a deep sense of knowing that place. I am currently considering the notions of fragility and impermanence within the natural world that surrounds me. Walking, observing, and gathering are rituals that require a commitment to careful observation; I slow down to comprehend the complexity of patterns, surfaces, and colors—the small, insignificant details. I work almost exclusively with vitreous enamel in combination with altered and textured metals; this medium allows me to explore ideas through the use of imagery and mark making. The techniques I work with give a tactile delicacy, and the marks I make create a language or code. It is an invented code, one that affords me a dialogue with the natural world. I aim to memorialize and commemorate the transience and sensual qualities of quotidian occurrences.

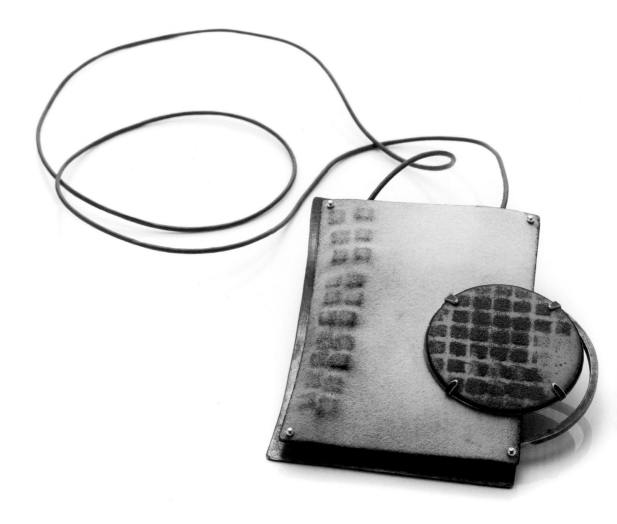

Jan Smith. "Street Walk" pendant. Fine-mesh-sifted vitreous enamel, chased copper, stenciled, hand-pierced and fabricated sterling silver, and leather cord. 2016. Photo: Gillean Proctor.

Artist Christine Dumont:

From a life rich in travels I've learned to pack light. Focusing on what was essential and really mattered was liberating. Art became essential, its exploration maintaining an anchor in my catalog of experiences. Over time, my sense of aesthetic changed and I saw my creative work evolve toward more streamlined forms, more economical lines, a reduced color palette. It dawned on me that this simplification was a metaphor for my aspiration to live an unencumbered life. This is when I knew what my voice was.

Simplicity is a hard design master. It can easily look shallow or empty. I seek the kind of simplicity that celebrates the line, the form, the texture—not annihilates them. I feel that simplicity gives my voice greater power. In this celebration, even the material must pull its weight. I now use pulverized rock as a base, held together by polymer.

But simplicity is also a good teacher. It gives me the discipline of saying no when the design doesn't quite work, and digging deeper for the reasons why. The deeper you dig, the more there is to dig. I've come to see design as a mystery to be lived, not a code to be cracked. This is also central to my voice.

Christine Dumont. "Rock Necklace." Pulverized rock, pigment, polymer clay, stainless steel, and sterling silver. 2018. Artist photo.

Artists Lisa and Scott Cylinder:

We began collaborating in 1988, and since then we have developed a wonderful exchange and interplay of ideas, concepts, and techniques. The common thread throughout our work has been a hunger to explore, utilize, and manipulate a multitude of materials. Often starting with found objects, we reinterpret these items, removing them from their original context. Our work displays a dichotomy of the man-made and natural worlds; how they intersect, weave, and parallel each other, which is apparent in our choices of both subject matter and materials. There is lightness to the themes and a sense of joy in our designs that comes from our love of making. We have a reverence and an overwhelming passion for handcraftsmanship.

Being that we are two people who see things differently, our ideas and sources are merged to create a single vision. From design through making, we ensure that both of our aesthetics are incorporated in this process and are always looking for that elusive inspiration from which our next concept will emerge.

Lisa and Scott Cylinder. "Crested Hornbill Saxophone Brooch." Vintage tenor saxophone key, sterling silver, brass, paduak wood, epoxy resin, lapis lazuli, Bakelite, and coral. Fabricated, cast, and carved. 2016. Photo: Scott Cylinder.

Artist Rebecca Thickbroom:

Early on, I struggled with my creativity. I set unrealistic deadlines and goals more appropriate to business projects than artistic ones. I just wanted to make some items to wear that week! But I came to realize that I needed to have patience with the design process and slow it down. My process developed into a kind of action-and-response system. Working directly with component parts, I try putting things together, then rearrange them, add new parts, and take away others. I began sharing design sketches with my art pals and started to discover my artistic voice. I realized how inspired I am by my homeland of Australia. I am passionate about all things coastal, native, and tribal. I realized that I had been collecting inspiration for years from my travels and interaction with the indigenous people of Australia, Africa, and Japan. These are the places where I always feel most alive and in harmony with the people and their environs. I'm confident about the road I'm on. I found my inspiration, process, and voice. I learned to "do me" and enjoy the journey.

Rebecca Thickbroom. "Raffia Sunset Rituals" pendant. Polymer, copper wire and sheet, artificial sinew, paint. 2015. Photo: Yeshen Venema.

Voice Exercise: Uncover Your Personal Themes

You are going to excavate your life and history to find out what gets you excited, what stirs your heart and memories, what makes you think, and what you are curious about. Begin by collecting fifteen to twenty images, or more. They can be actual photos of your home and family, as well as images from books and magazines. All the photos should arouse some deep feelings of connection. Whether on a spiritual, physical, intellectual, or philosophical level, they should be your unique interests.

Organize these images into groups with some commonality. They can be grouped by visual cues—colors, texture, or form, or organized in emotional groups—they make you feel happy, sad, lonely, or peaceful. Ask yourself, What am I responding to in this picture? Is it my heart, head, or soul reacting to each image?

Make notes about your reactions. Move things around. Regroup the pictures on the basis of different criteria. And keep asking questions. What is it about these images and groups of images that make you want to look deeper? What questions make you curious to know more? What are you discovering about yourself? Look for threads of connection and follow them.

This exercise can uncover your individuality. Take the time to follow your own trail of bread crumbs. It will lead you to discover that you have an interesting and unique voice, and you do indeed have much to say.

CRITIQUE

The most valuable skill I learned in art school was how to give and receive critique. Without the ability to analyze your work, your growth will be limited. Without the vocabulary to describe what you wish to accomplish, you won't be able to find solutions, and no one will be able to help you. Formal analysis is how we assimilate the concepts and terminology of art and design. The understanding of the elements and principles of design will become part of you, your work will mature, and your inspiration, voice, and intention will deepen.

In order to develop a good critical eye, you must do three things: separate your creative self from your analytical self, learn from your less successful pieces, and ask for objective opinions.

When you are creating, you should be in the zone, experimenting, taking risks, stretching your artistic muscles. You should be in love with what you are making and experiencing the joy of possibilities. But eventually you have to switch gears. Put on your analyst hat and specs and turn a critical eye on the work. Think like an editor. Be judicious and cool headed. Examine your creation. Did you end up where you intended, or did you get lost? Shifting your paradigm from maker to critic is a skill. It must be learned and practiced, and for some of us that's not easy. To grow yourself and your art, you need to learn to separate yourself from the work. It's not you—it's the stuff you make. Once you make this shift, you will be able to analyze your jewelry designs more objectively. Then when things go bad—and they sometimes

will—you will be able to find help, get answers, and learn from the experience.

Critiques help broaden our verbal skills. We learn to articulate our choices and talk about our art intelligently with customers, friends, and other artists. Imagine confidently joining in a conversation about why you do what you do, and understanding your peers when they do the same. They say, "You have to name it to claim it." Honing our verbal and analytical skills allows us claim our artistic identity.

Start by finding a critique buddy or group. It doesn't have to be another jeweler, and it doesn't have to be in person. There are a lot of virtual groups by medium or discipline on the internet. Choose a critique pal whom you trust and who respects you, and who understands your work and what you do. Look for artists who are at a similar artistic maturity level and ability, so that it is a group of your peers. Above all, look for critique pals who are genuinely interested in helping each other grow.

Myung Urso. "Plateau" brooch. Hand-dyed cotton, thread, Asian ink, sterling silver, and lacquer. 2018. Artist photo.

Next, set some ground rules about how the critique should progress and how to discuss the art in question. Agree that this is a reciprocal situation, that both parties will benefit from the experience, and that each has the other's best interest at heart. A critique session is giving and receiving for both parties, not a lecture or diatribe.

GIVING CRITIQUE

If you are going to be critiquing someone else's work, it helps to know where they're coming from.

Have the artist explain their intention. It will help both parties to understand what the artist wanted to achieve before beginning. If what they say doesn't align with what you see, that becomes a good place to start the conversation. Critique is about helping the other artist grow. You need to know the destination in order to give the right directions. Take a moment to carefully consider the artwork before you discuss it. Examine it. Keep an attitude of empathy and respect. Critique the artwork exactly as it is, not the way you would have done it. You are giving feedback about the art in the present moment, so stay present. And remember, critique isn't approval. Just saying you love the piece doesn't help anyone.

Analyze the composition. Be descriptive and specific. Explain what you see, using design terminology. Separate the principles and elements and discuss the shapes, rhythm, lines, contrast, and sensory qualities used in the work. Interpret the thoughts and feelings you have experiencing the piece. Seek to understand the meaning of the work.

Next, move into the constructive criticism. If you think certain aspects of a design aren't working, try to explain why. Ask questions and offer suggestions on how the piece could be improved. Asking questions will help the artist see problems they may not have noticed on their own. Share your experience with techniques or problems you have faced and solutions you tried. This should be a dialogue. Often, getting the artist to talk about their work allows them to discover solutions for themselves.

Don't be vague. It isn't helpful to say, "Something is just not right." If you can't be specific, it's better not to say anything at all. On the other hand, if you have a gut feeling about it, do your best to figure it out what it is, so you can help.

Anne Havel. "Wrinkle" bracelet. Vitreous enamel on copper. 2018. Artist photo.

Limit the use of personal pronouns, to make sure the critique is about the design and not about the maker. In other words, say, "I like the contrast between the smooth and rough textures" rather than "I like how you contrasted the smooth and rough textures." We all feel personally connected to our work, but in a critique it is best to separate the person from the piece. Keep it short. Say what you have to say and then stop. Droning on and on will muddle the information, and its impact will be lost.

Remember that you are on the same side, that you are evaluating the work together. This means asking the artist questions and listening to them critique their own work.

The goal is to help the artist improve. If you aim for that, you'll get it right.

The design may not be to your taste, but the other person deserves honest feedback. Put yourself in their shoes. If someone is brave enough to share their work and ask for feedback, then they deserve to get an honest assessment, both good and bad.

In the end, repeat or elaborate on what you liked about the piece so that the critique ends on a positive note. This way, the artist leaves knowing that although the piece needs some reworking, there is plenty of good design already.

RECEIVING CRITIQUE

Let's hope that your critique pal will follow these guidelines and you will have a potent, honest critique. What is your role in this dyad? To get the most from this experience, it's just as important that you follow some guidelines too.

Clearly state what you hope to get from the critique. Let the others know what you were trying to accomplish in the current work. Listen attentively. Consider how the work comes across to someone not as personally involved as you are. There are no categorical right and wrong answers, only a variety of subjective views that vary from one artist to the next.

With cool detachment, hear the critical points and consider them with an open mind. You may need time to absorb the feedback before you decide what to do about it. So listen carefully to what your critique buddy has to say. Avoid interrupting or contradicting the appraisal; the other person has taken

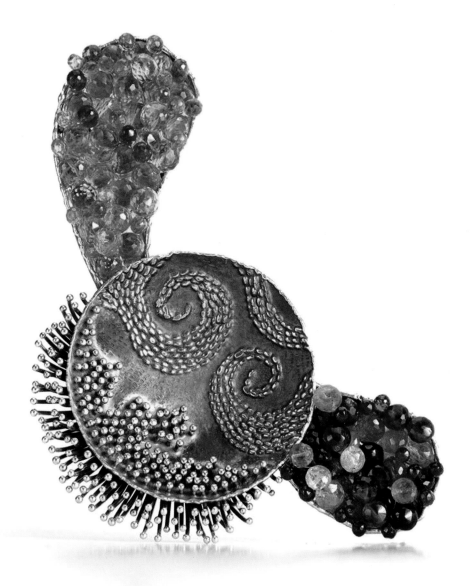

So Young Park. "Moon Wings" brooch. Oxidized silver, tourmaline, citrine, and garnet. 2017. Artist photo.

time to engage with your work, and they deserve your patience and respect.

Remember that the critique is about making the work the best it can be. This is not personal. It's not about your character, talents, or abilities. Don't be defensive. Defensiveness is adversarial and will shut down further discussion. Stay neutral and you will have a deeper discussion and better mutual understanding. This is a process that aims to improve the trajectory of your art, and you are getting the help of someone who deals with the same issues you do.

When the critique is over, take time to reflect. Let all the impressions and ideas sink in before deciding what to act on. It will take time to find your way forward in changing the design. It is fantastic to get someone else's input, but you don't want to simply substitute their judgment for your own. Implement the changes you decide on, and if necessary, ask for further feedback.

Five-Step Critique

1. Discover the artist's intention: Listen closely while the maker describes the ideas or concepts they were working with. Ask questions about the work and the artist to gain clarity and understanding.

2. Describe the work: Using specific design vocabulary, tell the artist what you see. Use descriptive words and adjectives. Talk about the use of form, movement, color, light and dark, texture, balance, and unity, for example. Explore the themes and construction together.

3. Interpret the work: Share your overall response to the piece. Balance the positives and negatives. Discuss your impressions, thoughts, and feelings. Explain and expand on your views in descriptive detail. Remember to talk about the work and not the person!

4. Evaluate the piece: Does it work? Has the artist achieved their intended goal? Ask questions and engage the artist in talking about their work. Suggest actionable steps based on the artist's goals and not your own.

5. Listen as much as you talk. Remember you are in this together. We are all trying to make better art all the time. Formal critique is not personal. To successfully and thoughtfully evaluate a design for yourself or others, address form, content, and intention.

Gallery

Julie Powell. "Diebenkorn Cuff—Urbana 62" bracelet. Glass
seed beads on monofilament. 2018. Photo: Larry Sanders.

Francesca Vitali. "Words and Black" bracelet. Repurposed paper and book pages. 2011. Artist photo.

Bettina Speckner. "Lady Vase" brooch. Ferrotype, silver, and diamonds. 2014. Artist photo.

Christel van der Laan. "Holier Than Thou" brooch. Ceramic honeycomb, powder-coated silver, and tabasco geodes. 2009. Photo: Adrian Lambert.

Danielle Embry. "In Your Prettiest Disguise" brooch. Enamel on copper, sterling silver, and monofilament. 2018. Artist photo.

Kaori Juzu. "For You, Jamie . . ." brooch. Enamel, steel, copper, and silver. 2016. Artist photo. Collection of Jamie Bennett, New York. Promised gift, Enamel Foundation, Los Angeles, California.

Rebecca Hannon. "Balloon Brooch." Laminate, silver, and horsehair. 2009. Artist photo.

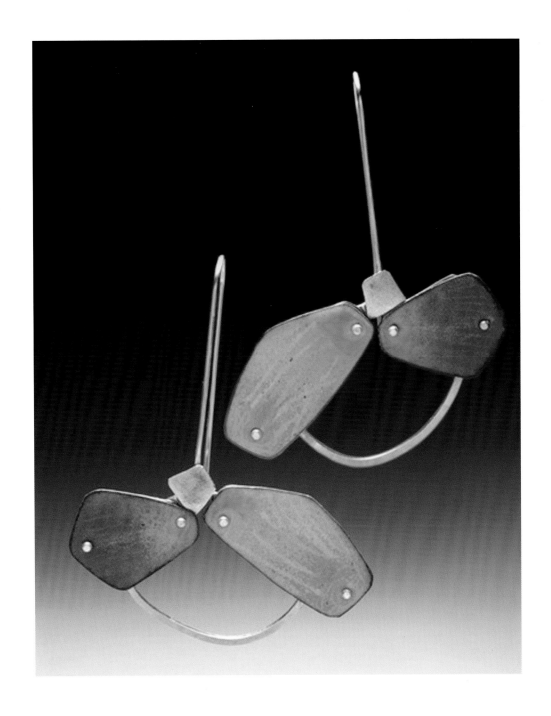

Lauren Pollaro. Earrings. Enamel on copper, brass, gold-filled
wire, and sterling silver. 2017. Photo: Charley Freiberg.

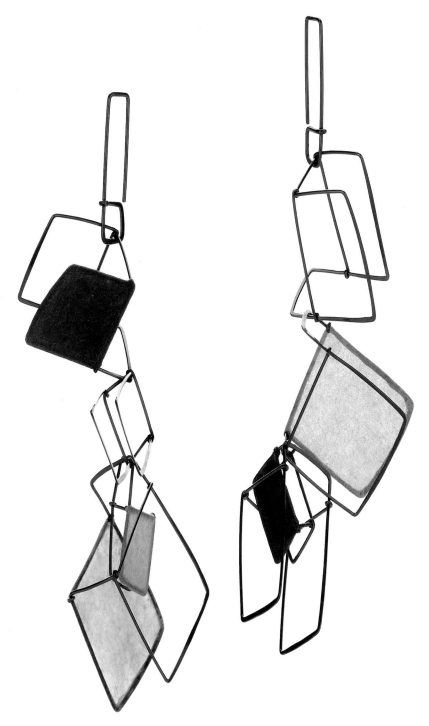

Tia Kramer. "Fluttering Earrings." Detachable from "Fluttering Necklace." Sterling and handmade paper. 2011. Photo: Hank Drew.

Anna Johnson. "Rerum Natura" necklace. Muskrat skull,
morganite, thulite, magnesite, fine and sterling silver, bronze, cast
sedum sarmentosum. 2018. Artist photo.

Brooke Marks-Swanson. "Tracings" collar. Knit leather, oxidized silver, pearls, and Japanese fiber. 2018. Photo: Jim Clemenson.

Opposite: Cynthia Toops. "Sketchbook" necklace. Micromosaic polymer clay, direct drawing on clay, drawing over transfers, hollow glass bead, and sterling. Glass beads by Dan Adams, and ceramic bead by Barnard Jones. 2018. Photo: Doug Yaple.

Loretta Lam. "Skipping Stones" necklace. Hollow-formed polymer beads, copper, rubber O-rings. 2015. Photo: Bob Barrett.

Tamara Grüner. "Carabus Auratus" neckpiece. Emerald, mother-of-pearl, gilded historical metal pieces, rhodanized silver, glass, plastic, paint, steel. 2017. Photo: Alexander König.

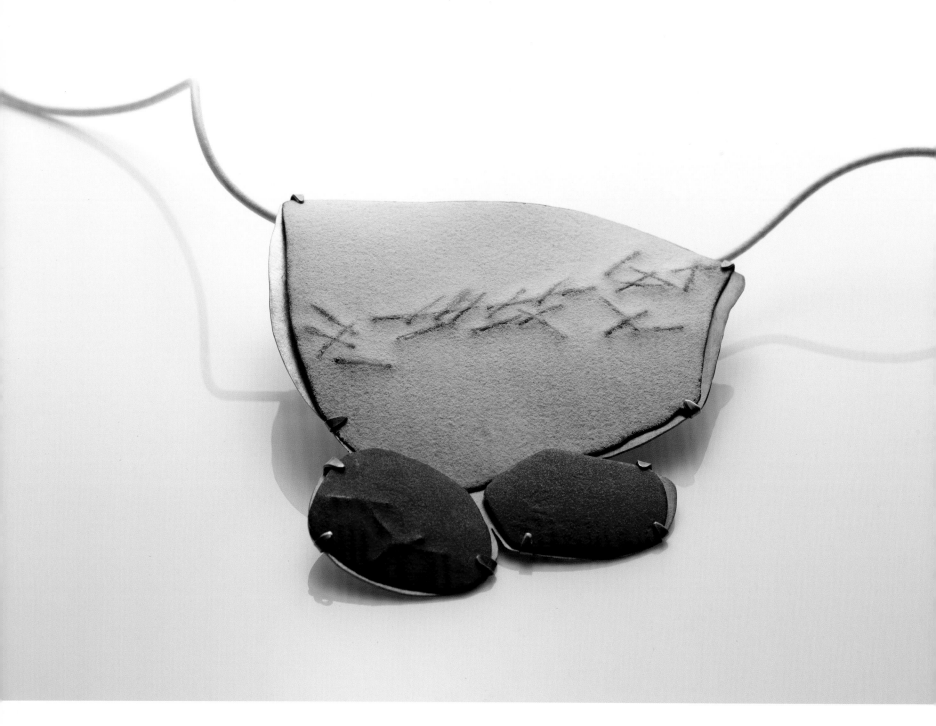

Jan Smith. "Sandstone Erosions" pendant. Fine-mesh-sifted vitreous enamel, chased copper, hand-pierced and fabricated sterling silver, and leather cord. 2016. Photo: Gillean Proctor.

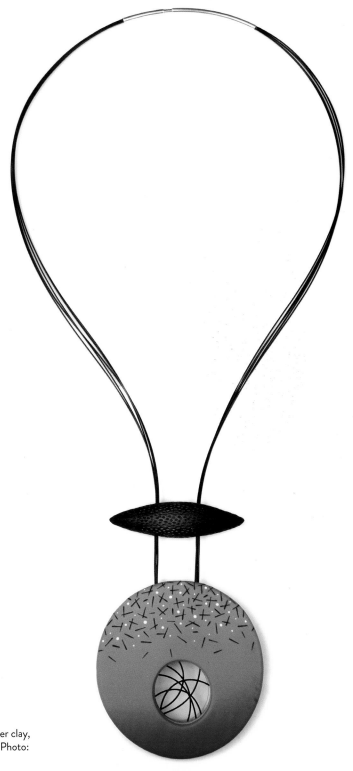

Jeffrey Lloyd Dever. "Fireflies at Dusk" pendant. Polymer clay, nylon-coated stainless-steel cable, sterling silver. 2018. Photo: Gregory R. Staley.

Julie Shaw. "Magical Sky" necklace. Sterling silver, 22 kt. gold, faceted lapis lazuli, enamel, and kyanite beads. 2016. Photo: Ryder Gledhill.

Allison Hilton Jones. "2 Balls" ring. Sterling silver, concrete, and felt. 2015. Photo: Cole Rodger.

Isabelle Posillico. "Satellite Aqua Ring." 18 kt. and 22 kt. gold, aquamarine, diamond, blue zircon, and green tourmaline. 2006. Photo: Hap Sakwa.

Jed Green. "Bud and Bloom" ring. Glass, paint, silver, and freshwater pearls. 2017. Photo: Tas Kyprianou.

BIBLIOGRAPHY

BOOKS

Aimone, Steven. *Design! A Lively Guide to Design Basics for Artists and Craftspeople.* New York: Lark Books, 2004.

Albers, Josef. *Interaction of Color.* New Haven, CT: Yale University Press, 2013. First published in 1963.

Arnheim, Rudolf. *Art and Visual Perception.* Berkeley and Los Angeles: University of California Press, 1974. First published in 1954.

Day, Lewis F. *Pattern Design.* Mineola, NY: Dover, 1999. First published in 1933.

Deeb, Margie. *The Beader's Guide to Jewelry Design.* New York: Lark Jewelry & Beading, 2014.

Glei, Jocelyn K., ed. *Manage Your Day-to-Day: Build Your Routine, Find Your Focus, and Sharpen Your Creative Mind.* Las Vegas, NV: Amazon, 2013.

Gonnella, Rose, and Max Friedman. *Design Fundamentals: Notes on Color Theory.* Berkeley, CA: Peachpit, 2014.

Kobayashi, Shigenobu. *Colorist: A Practical Handbook for Personal and Professional Use.* Tokyo, New York, and London: Kodansho International, 1998.

Olver, Elizabeth. *The Art of Jewelry Design from Idea to Reality.* London: Quarto, 2001.

Rose, Augustus, and Antonio Cirino. *Jewelry Making and Design.* New York: Dover, 1967.

Sprintzen, Alice. *Jewelry: Basic Techniques and Design.* Radnor, PA: Chilton Book, 1980.

Untracht, Oppi. *Jewelry Concepts and Technology.* New York: Doubleday, 1982.

Von Neumann, Robert. *The Design and Creation of Jewelry.* Radnor, PA: Chilton Book, 1961.

E-BOOKS

Fox, Connie. *Maker Magic.* San Diego, CA: Connie Fox, 2014. www.jatayu.com/maker-magic-book-by-connie-fox/.

WEBSITES

Anapur, Eli. "The Importance of Balance in Art." Widewalls, September 17, 2016. www.widewalls.ch/balance-in-art-symmetrical-asymmetrical-radial-blance-design/.

Bartel, Marvin. "Empathic Critique." Art & Learning to Think & Feel, March 15, 2017. http://bartelart.com/arted/critique08.html.

Bradley, Steven. "Design Principles: Compositional Flow and Rhythm." *Smashing Magazine*, April 29, 2015.

Accessed October 28, 2018. www.smashingmagazine.com/2015/04/design-principles-compositional-flow-and-rhythm.

Bradley, Steven. "Dominance: Creating Focal Points in Your Design." Vanseo Design, February 1, 2010. http://vanseodesign.com/web-design/dominance/.

"Color Theory—Color as Emotion." Artyfactory, October 13, 2018. Accessed October 28, 2018. www.artyfactory.com/color_theory/color_theory_3.htm.

Dellorco, Chris. "Art vs. Commerce: The Artist's Eternal Conflict." *Art Business News*, March 5, 2013. https://artbusinessnews.com/2013/03/art-vs-commerce-the-artists-eternal-conflict/.

"Emotional and Psychological Meaning of Colours." MyLifeMyStuff, April 28, 2012. Accessed October 28, 2018. https://mylifemystuff.wordpress.com/2012/04/26/emotional-and-psychological-meaning-of-colours/.

Esaak, Shelley. "How Are Patterns Used in Art?" ThoughtCo, April 12, 2018. www.thoughtco.com/pattern-definition-in-art-182451.

Flye, Robert. "Repetition, Rhythm and Pattern." Flyeschool, 2011. http://flyeschool.com/content/repetition-rhythm-and-pattern.

Fussell, Matt. "Color Theory—the Elements of Art." The Virtual Instructor, September 22, 2018. https://thevirtualinstructor.com/Color.html.

Goss, Simon. "A History of Jewellery." Victoria and Albert Museum. www.vam.ac.uk/articles/a-history-of-jewellery.

Henry, Todd. "The 4 Phases of Developing Your Creative Voice." 99U, August 20, 2015. https://99u.adobe.com/articles/51575/the-4-phases-of-developing-your-creative-voice.

Hurst, Ashley. "Proportion—a Principle of Art." *TheVirtualInstructor Blog.* The Virtual Instructor, May 14, 2018. https://thevirtualinstructor.com/blog/proportion-a-principle-of-art.

Lamp, Lucy. "Design in Art: Repetition, Pattern and Rhythm." Sophia. www.sophia.org/tutorials/design-in-art-repetition-pattern-and-rhythm.

Lamp, Lucy. "Elements of Art: Shape." Sophia. www.sophia.org/tutorials/elements-of-art-shape.

Lee, Patina. "The Importance of Pattern in Art." Widewalls, August 8, 2016. www.widewalls.ch/pattern-in-art/.

"Line as a Visual Element of Art." Artyfactory, October 13, 2018. www.artyfactory.com/art_appreciation/visual-elements/line.html.

McIntyre, Carol. "How Do Artists Know If a Color Is Warm or Cool? Important Color Theory Tip—Celebrating Color." Celebrating Color, November 2, 2016. www.celebratingcolor.com/is-a-color-is-warm-or-cool-important-color-theory/.

McNee, Lori. "Use the Hidden Meaning of Color in Your Art." Lori McNee Art & Fine Art Tips, August 26, 2018. www.fineart-tips.com/2009/08/use-the-hidden-meaning-of-color-in-your-art/.

Popova, Maria. "Fixed vs. Growth: The Two Basic Mindsets That Shape Our Lives." Brain Pickings, September 23, 2018. Accessed October 28, 2018. www.brainpickings.org/2014/01/29/carol-dweck-mindset/.

"Session 2: Principles of Design; Contrast." Moodle Group Public Hub, hub.rockyview.ab.ca/mod/book/view.php?id=2706&chapterid=2418.

Taheri, Maryam. "10 Basic Elements of Design." Creative Market, June 29, 2018. https://creativemarket.com/blog/10-basic-elements-of-design.

Williams, Lianne. "How to Give CONSTRUCTIVE Criticism to ARTISTS." Lianne Williams. liannewilliams.com/blog/how-to-give-constructive-criticism-to-an-artist.

INDEX

Loretta Lam is an award-winning artist and well-known studio jeweler whose work is found in fine galleries and top art fairs nationwide. She has a BFA in silversmithing and has been working in polymer since 1999. Lam is an internationally recognized teacher and speaker who regularly presents workshops in jewelry design and technique. Her work has been showcased in many books and magazines and has been included in numerous prestigious exhibitions, including CraftForms International, the Smithsonian Craft Show, and Artistar Jewels International, Milan. She lives and works in Carmel, New York.